Aquarius
The Age of Revelation, Choice and Transformation

ALSO BY PAULINE EDWARD

Gateway to a New World

The Healing of Humanity

The Movement of Being

Choosing the Miracle

Leaving the Desert: Embracing the Simplicity of A Course in Miracles

Making Peace with God: The Journey of a Course in Miracles Student

Astrological Crosses: Exploring the Cardinal, Fixed and Mutable Modes

The Power of Time: Understanding the Cycles of Your Life's Path

L'Hermès: Dictionnaire des correspondances symboliques, with Marc Bériault and Axel Harvey

AQUARIUS
THE AGE OF REVELATION, CHOICE AND TRANSFORMATION

Pauline Edward

Desert Lily Publications
Montreal, Canada

Copyright © 2021 Pauline Edward
Published by Desert Lily Publications, Montreal, Canada
All rights reserved. No part of this work may be reproduced or used in any form or by any means, electronic, digital or mechanical, including photocopying, recording or any retrieval system, without the prior written permission of the publisher.

Paperback ISBN 978-1-927694-07-7
Hardcover ISBN 978-1-927694-16-9

Cover design, photography, layout and illustrations: Pauline Edward
Poems by Michael J. Miller, used by permission
Editorial consultation: Veronica Schami

Contents

Preface vii
1. Let There Be Light 1
2. Doorway to a New Age 13
3. Breaking the Cycle 31
4. Standing on the Threshold 47
5. More than This 63
6. Beyond Beliefs 81
7. An Island Adventure 99
8. Homeward Bound 117
9. Awakening to Oneness 135
10. The Creative Power of Mind 153
11. Higher Ground 171
12. A New Beginning 187
Bibliography 201
About the Author 202
Reviews 203

Preface

> We begin the journey back by setting out TOGETHER, and gather in our brothers (and sisters) as we CONTINUE together. Every gain in our strength is offered for all, so they, too, can lay aside their weakness and add their strength to us. (ACIM, Ch. 8. p. 184)

We Journey Together

Throughout my life, writing has served as an integral part of my learning process. It's almost as though putting the words on paper makes it real for me—well, on a computer screen and then on a USB key, a backup drive, a printed page for my binder and, just for good measure, a second backup drive, sometimes a third—I wouldn't want to lose one word of that precious insight. Writing functions as an anchor of sorts, marking the progress, clarifying the issues, making the questions and answers relevant—at least the writing part, more than the obsessive backups part. In over half a century, many words have been captured—the large pile of notebooks, loose-leaf pages, discs and drives being a testament to that fact. And so, as writing seems to be a significant part of my journey, I continue to put ink to paper and, of course, bits and bytes onto drives.

Besides my astrology and numerology books, *Astrological Crosses* and *The Power of Time*, this is the sixth book in which I share my seemingly insatiable quest to uncover the true meaning of life, in particular, the journey of awakening. Perhaps I should say my quest for a full experience of the truth because I have come to "understand" that intellectual understanding, no matter how comprehensive—although a valuable part of the journey—is meaningless without the confirmation of that "inner knowing." The books leading up to this one describe a search that began with the traditional Roman Catholic doctrines of my youth, moving on through Eastern, metaphysical, theosophical, occult, shamanic, esoteric and New Age teachings and eventually to *A Course in Miracles* (ACIM, the Course).

While this book will cover some of the topics explored in the previous books, they will be presented in a different manner and then further developed. I have found that hearing or reading the same message in different words, at a different time or within a different context can trigger sudden flashes of understanding. Very often, it is these simple, sometimes unexpected flashes that make the learning and understanding meaningful. Also, this book is different from the previous books in that the guidance received has been mostly integrated with the writing. Although I continue to join with guidance, the goal is to learn to work in union with guidance and to connect with the inner Voice, the true Self or the I Am, so we can bridge the gap of separation and experience our Oneness with All that is.

Astrology came into my life over fifty years ago, at the start of my quest to uncover the meaning of life, a story shared in *Making Peace with God*. My studies and consultation practice have provided me with a unique perspective on the journey of humanity throughout the Ages. This perspective can be helpful in understanding where we are now and how to proceed in order to make the changes that humanity is calling forth at this time.

As we leave behind the Era of Pisces and transition into the Era of Aquarius, we move into new territory for which we do not have a clearly defined roadmap. Given that we are shifting into what appears to be unknown territory, it is essential that we develop our innate ability to gauge what is valid and what is not valid, what is relevant and what is not relevant and, most importantly, what is meant for us and what is not meant for us. Fortunately, clarity of perception and intelligent discernment is very much in harmony with the climate of Aquarius.

PREFACE

As expressed in *The Healing of Humanity*, there are as many paths Home as paths that lead away from Home. So, in the matter of emerging consciousness or awakening, there is no one-size-fits-all formula. By the same token, if a particular path appeals to you, it does not make you any more likely to experience awakening than one for whom that path holds no appeal. Whether it includes a spiritual component or not, any path that leads to the full conscious awareness of Being is worthy of attention.

This book presents one perspective, one person's perspective of the shift. Each person will have their own unique perspective since each person's experience will be unique. Please note that the teachings that have been appropriate for me are mentioned for reference purposes only and should not be taken as the only way. There are many wonderful new teachings emerging today as humanity calls out for more. Ultimately, all teachings that reveal truth—whether ancient, traditional or contemporary—will meet on some level.

Furthermore, as we will see, the purpose of a teaching is not to fill a void or a lack. A worthy teaching will shed light and help us uncover our current level of knowing and, in so doing, will clear the way for our next step. What truly matters is the experience of the light, the wisdom and the unconditional love that guides our Being, something that can and will ultimately be achieved while going about our normal daily activities.

Although this is the sixth book on the subject of awakening to higher consciousness, it is not necessary to have read the first five before reading this one. While it includes a few references to previous works, it addresses the subject from a different perspective and is meant to stand on its own. If this book has called to you and you wish to skip over the previous ones, jump right in. Nowhere does it say that everyone must get on the train at the same station; you get on the train at the stop nearest you. Only the destination is the same for everyone—removing the barriers to the full conscious experience of Being.

These writings express snippets of one person's life-long spiritual journey; however, it does not mean that others must pursue the same path. Thank goodness! To do so would likely add unnecessary length to a journey that need not be more than a moment in time. For, how long does it take to turn within to where truth awaits? As long as it seemed, this journey was appropriate for me; it was simply shared for those who are curious about another seeker's experience. Ultimately, your journey—each person's journey—is unique because each person is a unique expression of the Life Principle.

Another reason for jumping right in is that this book is written in a way that might be more relatable for people who are not particularly "religious" or into spirituality or metaphysics but who are nonetheless curious and ready to explore what might lie beyond the current boundaries of human understanding and knowledge. As a way of providing a different frame of reference, it places the current shift of consciousness—or awakening—in the context of the transition from the Age of Pisces to the Age of Aquarius.

The Age of Aquarius has a very different climate or vibration than that of the Age of Pisces. This is causing many to question and wonder and reach out for answers. So it is that many new teachings are emerging, while significant clarifications and updates are being brought to ancient and traditional teachings. As we will see, concepts, terminology and language that may have been suitable in the past, as is commonly found in traditional spiritual, metaphysical or religious teachings, may need a little updating in the new climate of Aquarius. Long-standing beliefs, as well as language, will be examined to ensure that they facilitate our growth and learning so we can experience this much-anticipated, and above all, much-needed, shift of consciousness.

Over the years, I have, on occasion, recommended *A Course in Miracles* and ACIM-related materials to friends and clients, a work that was most helpful on my journey. I can honestly say that very few have reported that they could appreciate, let alone understand, this work. I know many people who are familiar with the Course, even own a copy, usually tucked away on a shelf collecting dust. A few have read some of it, but more often than not, most have never gotten beyond the first few pages. As I was working on this section,

PREFACE

one of my clients shared how she had purchased a copy, tried to read it, shrugged, immediately closed it, and never gave it another glance. When I asked one client, an avid three-year Course student, to explain the meaning of the "miracle," I was met by a bewildered look, a couple of ers and ums, but no answer. I've met only a couple of people who were so blown away after having read the book that they went back to the beginning to do it all over again.

During this highly significant time of shift for humanity, much is being revealed about who and what we are. What is interesting is the unique way in which different teachings can present the same core messages. This book will explore some of the essential elements of these teachings as they relate to the current shift in consciousness. The aim is to sow the seeds of curiosity in those who are beginning to wonder if there might be more to life. In so doing, they may begin to discover that there is far more to who and what we are than what we have been taught up until now.

Humanity is crying out for more; humanity is ready for more, and so it is that humanity is being gifted with more. Fortunately, teachings are being made available in today's language so they can easily be implemented in our lives. Right now, the world needs "miracles"—major shifts in consciousness or corrections to our perception of life. The world needs those who, having eagerly embraced this shift within themselves, will go out into the world, engage in their normal daily activities, all the while embodying a new message by being the intelligent, and always appropriate, presence of love, no matter the circumstance.

If you are reading this book, chances are that you have not yet experienced full conscious awareness. You may be curious about how others are faring on their journey, or you may be looking for insights that may inspire you and help facilitate your journey. Due to the radical nature of the shift of consciousness facing humanity at this time, as we travel this unfamiliar path, it can be helpful to know that we are not alone and that there are indeed others who share our deep desire for a greater experience of Being. Rest assured, we are not alone.

As we will see, the journey is made easier for everyone as more brothers and sisters join in. Ultimately, we are in this together. So thank you to those who are brave enough to undertake this journey. In so doing, you—we—each in our own unique way, contribute to the shift in consciousness that will light the way for every living being on planet Earth.

If you are awake and happen to be reading this book—and I welcome and feel your presence as I write these words—there is no doubt that you will express compassion and support for our valiant efforts. We are open to receiving your help as we seek to uncover the truth and experience what lies beyond the boundaries of the current human condition. You will send thoughts of encouragement and maybe even stand and applaud us for our bravery and dedication on our journeys. And since minds are joined, those loving thoughts will be well-received by us stirring sleepers. For your loving support, for your continued gifts of insight, we are eternally grateful.

Another reason to keep writing, or more precisely publishing, is for my readers since I can write without publishing. At a writers' group meeting, we were asked to take a few minutes and write anything that came to mind. Not one to be comfortable "writing on demand," I tucked away my timidity, turned to the small voice within, and scribbled out the following:

> What is this thing called writing? It is like the breath of my being seeking expression wanting only to be set free, without reservation, without expectation. It is the liberation of my soul, its blossoming into fullness, taking its place in this universe of infinite possibilities.
>
> Although not necessary, feedback from readers today has been received as a blessing. It seems that my sharing of this journey of unfolding has been helpful for them too. In this way, writing ultimately flows in two directions: outward from my soul and back to me from the soul of my reader. The journey of writing is thus made complete.

PREFACE

A while back, I received an email from a reader asking if there was another book on the way. If only for one reader, as a writer, and as one who is only too happy to serve, how could I say no? And so, I wish to express my deepest gratitude to those who have taken the time to share how helpful my books have been for them. Writing has long been and may continue to be a part of my function in this life. From guidance, I will take my cues.

This book might have been subtitled *The Continuing Chronicles of a Recalcitrant Sleeper, Why Make the Journey Any Longer than Necessary, Why We Don't Really Want to Wake Up* or *How Radical Do We Dare to Be*. Feel free to make up your own. Our perceptions, interpretations, learning and understanding are unique, as are our journeys and experiences. Like you, I wish to wake up and experience the fullness of my Being as well as the unique fullness of everyone and everything I encounter at every moment. We are now being invited to abandon our old learning and choose something new—a revolutionary new conscious awareness for humanity—which is what we hope to explore in this book. With renewed peaceful dedication, we forge ahead.

A Little Help from Above

Some of my readers have expressed that what they like most about my books are the personal stories. I must admit that there aren't many stories at this time in my life, at least not big, dramatic, exciting ones—not that there ever were any. Besides, as a writer, I am quite content to hide behind my pen and paper, well, my computer. My life is simple, peaceful and serves mainly as a means to an end, though perhaps a somewhat different end than it once served. But, my inner voice nudges me to share my story, and so I oblige. Your life and that of every brother and sister is also a story, for each is an expression of Life, so each story is worthy of love and attention. Here's one story I can share to get us started, which for me, once again, reinforced my function as a writer.

One day I went for a walk to test a new raincoat. It was raining steadily, so perfect weather for testing the impermeability of the coat. I had learned that "water-resistant" was not quite the same as "waterproof"; I was in search of the latter. I grabbed my knapsack, threw in my recorder—just in case I should get some insights—snatched my keys and headed out into the rain. After a good 4 km walk, I was very pleased to conclude that my new coat was effectively waterproof. Unfortunately, to my great chagrin, I learned that my knapsack was not; it had soaked up rainwater like a thirsty sponge. I pulled out a packet of tissues, and, even in plastic wrapping, the tissues were soaked. I panicked as I reached for my recorder. Immediately, I pressed the Play button; it whirled a couple of times and then died.

My heart sank. This little device was essential to my writing process, as I use it to grab insights and guidance whenever I am not at the computer. Of course, these priceless insights never come when I'm sitting in front of the computer; that would be too easy. Rather, they come in the middle of the night, in the wee small hours of the morning or while out walking. So I keep the recorder by my side at all times, just in case. Many years ago, I had suffered from an excruciatingly painful frozen shoulder. I developed the practice of recording my notes and insights. Then, while playing the recorded material, I dictate it into my word processor with the help of a speech recognition program. That's my process for the first draft. It may sound complicated, but it works. It is much kinder for the health of my arms and shoulders than typing out thousands of words. Since writing is rewriting, this process significantly reduces keyboard time.

There were over fifty entries on the recorder that day, more than I usually collect before unloading. Even if the entries were brief, these snippets were the raw material I use for writing. Over fifty entries—gone! I pressed the Play button again—nothing. I replaced the batteries with new ones and pressed Play—nothing. I was devastated. I took a long, deep breath and chose to be at peace. I resigned myself to the fact that if these entries were necessary for my writing or simply for my well-being, I would receive the help I needed.

PREFACE

On a hunch, not quite ready to give up, I grabbed a plastic bag, scooped in some rice and dropped the recorder in the bag. At least one thing I had seen on television might come in handy. I tested the recorder several times over the next couple of hours. Each time it just whirled and died. Eventually, I pressed Play and managed to hear one of fifty-five entries, which I immediately dictated into the notes file. Again I pressed Play, but the device whirled and died. After several attempts, I accepted that the material on the recorder would probably not be available. It was lost.

Before going to bed that night, I prayed to our buddies "out there," our awakened friends who always remain ready to help should we dare to reach out and ask for help. If this material was essential to my writing, it would be available. One last press of the Play button—nothing. The recorder was dead. I took another deep breath and called it a night. The next morning, the first thing I did as I stepped out of bed was to reach for the recorder. I pressed Play. It worked! I ran to the computer, played all remaining fifty-four entries, one after the other, dictating them into my doc file, and of course, making the required backups and printouts along the way. Once the last entry had been transcribed, saved and printed, the device whirled a couple of times and died. That was it. I had been able to recover several days of recorded material. Relieved and profoundly grateful, I went online and ordered a new recorder. The message was loud and clear: time to get back to writing.

Thank You

I would like to express my heartfelt gratitude for the tremendous help we are receiving during this time of change on planet Earth. So many teachers and helpers are stepping forth and providing us with the knowledge we need to make this shift as smooth as possible.

Not only are we sent teachers when we are ready to learn, we are also sent friends with whom to share the journey. A big thank you to all who have provided support for my writing efforts: Helena, Pooran, Epp and Camille. Thank you Mike Miller for helping with the edits and for sharing your wonderful poems. And, of course, thank you Veronica Schami for your editorial wisdom.

Also, thank you to my clients for asking those questions that push me to find answers to what seem like unanswerable questions, and for sharing the beauty of the unfolding of your Being.

Thank you, thank you, thank you.

CHAPTER 1

Let There Be Light

Health depends on being in harmony with our souls… We each have a Divine mission in this world, and our souls use our minds and bodies as instruments to do this work, so that when all three are working in unison the result is perfect health and perfect happiness. (*Free Thyself*, Dr. Edward Bach)

I Could Write a Book… Uh, Maybe Later

In the summer of 2019, when I told my friend Helena that I had started to work on another book, she asked, "What will you write about?" Honestly, I had no idea, and I was very much okay with that. "I'm not awake," I replied. "So, I gotta keep going." In recent years, I have come to appreciate that, at least for me, writing opens the way for the inner voice of my soul as well as for that precious connection with guidance. Having learned that this journey cannot be undertaken alone, there was no stopping now, or so I thought.

There was never any doubt that I would always journal and gather notes, whether to give way to inner guidance or to capture insights from the higher Self, okay, and maybe the occasional tiny bit of venting. But I did wonder if *The Healing of Humanity* might have been my last published work. As much as I tried, I simply could not see a clear direction for another book. Hadn't all been said? Did I have anything new to contribute? Was anyone actually interested in my musings? Yet, that persistent inner voice nudged me to continue, pointing out that the notes I was gathering would be helpful for other souls on the journey.

Early one morning, I grabbed the recorder and caught the following insight: "It is becoming clear now, today, at this moment, that I may be ready to write another book. It's not that I have a book 'in me,' but I will allow a book to come 'through me.' This relieves me of the pressure of being the author of a book; rather, I am a vehicle for the transmission of a book." That was back in January 2018. And so, despite not having a clear direction, basically not knowing what I was supposed to write about, I continued to gather notes, trusting that I would be guided when the time was right.

In the preface of *The Healing of Humanity*, I shared how distraction had hijacked my attention as soon as I started working on the book. Did I encounter resistance this time around? Well, yes, and no. If writing allows me to connect with guidance and inspiration—a connection I deeply cherish—why would there be resistance to writing another book? For a student of *A Course in Miracles*, an initial response might be to chalk up the resistance to the ego, that aspect of self that will not support what will ultimately lead to its undoing. Those familiar with this journey are aware of how fiercely this small self will resist the shift toward awakening, something it will do with surprising cleverness and creativity. And so, this was true to a certain extent.

But this time around, it was not so much resistance as a necessary timeout while I fine-tuned my learning. Despite that I believed to have, once again, found the ultimate teaching in *A Course in Miracles*, there would be more teachings to be explored. This idea of an "ultimate teaching" is a deeply ingrained pattern that had been played out many times throughout my life. Whenever I encountered a teaching to my liking, I would assume that that would be the end of it. No more need for learning; I had found the truth. Well, not quite, for, as *A Course in Miracles* says, "This course is a beginning, not an end," and so the journey continues.

Despite having often wondered when this lifelong quest would end, I would discover that learning was an ongoing, never-ending aspect of the life experience. As an expression of Source, Being is in constant movement, and learning is a natural by-product of this

CHAPTER 1 • LET THERE BE LIGHT

movement. This means that, at times, some past learning—especially irrelevant, redundant or outdated beliefs—may need to be released to make room for the new. Fortunately, for someone not really interested in taking on yet another course of study, I was shown that true knowledge comes from within. Teachings only help facilitate learning by supporting and validating our understanding as we move through the experiences encountered in the school of life.

While waiting for clarity on how and when to proceed with this book, I engaged in my favourite activities. Doing something you love is very centring, and so when not busy with consultation work, I listened to lectures while experimenting in the kitchen. As the weeks turned into months, I became somewhat of an expert on vegan cheesecakes, tweaking my recipes to increase the protein, reduce costs and simplify preparation. I experimented with flavours, including cranberry, blueberry, chocolate and matcha. Fortunately, I have neighbours who are only too eager to test my creations. One morning, when I messaged my young upstairs neighbour that I had a slice of mango coconut cheesecake for his lunch, he was at my door in forty-five seconds, barefoot, still in his pyjamas, holding up an empty plate. I think he may have teleported down from the fourth floor. When I had exhausted my creative options with cheesecakes—except perhaps a mochaccino version and maybe a maple one—I returned my attention to the book. Still, nothing was clear; the book project remained on hold.

At the start of 2019, I had the most unusual urge to purchase a piano. After a second client shared a positive experience with online piano lessons, I thought, why not. Whereas throughout the difficult years of my youth, books had been my friends, music had been my medicine. My younger brother was a gifted pianist, and my father was a fabulous guitarist, but all I could play was vinyl on the turntable. While I may have felt somewhat intimidated by the talent around me, that didn't stop me from listening. I dove into jazz and blues, enjoying everything from Stan Getz to Sonny Terry and Brownie McGee, the classics, from Chopin to Rachmaninoff, and the occasional Bach Cello Suites, just to get my thinking straight. There was nothing like a shot of Rachmaninoff's Piano Concerto No. 2 to uncork deep-seated emotions, although Piano Concerto No. 3 did a fine job too, as did the beautiful Diana Ross singing "Good Morning Heartache" or "God Bless the Child." Admittedly, I have odd musical tastes; but the fact remains that music was—and still is—such wonderful medicine.

Apparently, I was now in need of medicine. Not that I had ever stopped listening to music; quite the contrary. There was always music playing in the background in my home, usually smooth jazz—does it get any smoother than Kenny Rankin?—and, of course, the Standards, my favourites of the last couple of decades. Who can resist Rod Stewart singing "The Very Thought of You"? So when I learned that a new session of beginner piano lessons was starting the following week, I got busy. There was research to be done on which piano I should buy, and then there was the matter of shuffling furniture around to fit the instrument in my closet-sized condo. In less than two weeks, I had begun my first piano lessons, there was a brand-new Yamaha P125 in my living room, and, strangely, the furniture managed to flow even better than before. Go figure; feng shui at its best!

By the winter of 2020, I had progressed through several online beginner jazz and blues piano courses, posted a mini-eBook of my cheesecake recipes on my blog, gathered up over 90,000 words of notes, written a preface and made a rough list of topics to be developed for the book. While the music and cheesecakes were doing rather well, such was not the case with the writing. I had collected a lot of notes but still did not see how to put it all together. There was no clear direction; something was missing.

Detour into Darkness

Then along came the global crisis known as COVID-19. As "normal" life came to a halt, like many, I headed to the Internet in search of information. What I discovered was that there was no shortage of information in today's world. Besides daily updates from our

CHAPTER 1 • LET THERE BE LIGHT

prime minister and the evening news, I listened to talks by scientists, traditional and non-traditional doctors, as well as messages from various channellers and spiritual teachers. I also stumbled across the rants of a few conspiracy theorists and, although some of what was being said was somewhat interesting, I decided that these were not for me. I was neither a scientist nor a medical professional, and therefore could not correctly distinguish fact from fiction. I needed to be able to discern for myself what information would be helpful for me.

I discovered that many of the teachings that have emerged since the turn of the century were very interesting, all the more so that they supported my insights on the shift from Pisces to Aquarius. A few of these messages even corroborated—nearly verbatim—items in the notes I had gathered over the past couple of years. However, while some of the material was in harmony with my current understanding, the more I delved into teachings on awakening or enlightenment, the more I became confused. There were disturbing discrepancies and outright contradictions among the works of popular teachers, which, even when allowing for variations in the use of language, context and terminology, simply could not be reconciled. As the weeks passed, I grew more confused than I had been in a very long time; in fact, I couldn't recall ever having been so confused.

Overwhelmed by doubt, I began to question everything I thought I knew and understood until one night, it all came to a crashing halt. The page I had been reading on the Internet suddenly disappeared. It was as though something in the heavens had cried STOP—and it stopped. All that remained was darkness. I had reached a point where I doubted everything I had ever studied, everything I had learned and believed, and worst of all, everything I had written about in my books. I doubted even the existence of God—the God with whom I had begun to enjoy a peaceful, loving connection. Nothing could be proved. Nothing could be validated. I was lost. Everything I had learned over a lifetime of study no longer made sense. Life no longer had meaning. Only darkness remained.

Indeed, I had fallen into a very dark funk. A trained astrologer would immediately recognize the pileup of planets in Capricorn transiting over Chiron (also known as the wounded healer) in the 12th house of my astrology chart, locking me into a dark, seemingly endless tunnel. I casually—or perhaps not so casually—refer to the 12th house as the house of garbage, that place where we shove stuff out of sight to be dealt with later. Judging by the mess in the dark tunnel, later had arrived, and it demanded attention. What was this thing called awakening, anyway? What was this nonsense about enlightenment? Had I wasted my entire life on a senseless quest? Who was I kidding! I was living in a world that was more insane than ever, I had lost faith in everything I thought I knew, and I couldn't see my way through the darkness.

As though it wasn't enough for my spirit to be blinded by confusion, the day following a Mother's Day online video dinner with my daughters, pain suddenly began to creep into my left shoulder and arm. During the day, the pain grew so intense that I could no longer use my arm. Desperate for relief but not inclined to make my way to the hospital during the pandemic, I called the emergency health line. I jotted down recommendations for pain relief medication as well as instructions for icing the affected area. Unable to go to the pharmacy, I reached out to a neighbour for help. Fortunately, she had the recommended items; no need to go to the store.

To add panic to pain, the ON Switch on my computer started to fail. A broken computer was the worst thing that could happen to a self-employed consultant and writer. My entire life was in that device. Although I had a backup PC on standby, I hadn't turned it on in quite a while. There was no guarantee that my software would work smoothly or that it actually would boot up since it too had suffered mechanical problems.

This was indeed a very dark tunnel, and there wasn't a song in the world that could relieve the anguish that infused every corner of my mind. I couldn't move, couldn't write and obviously, couldn't practise the piano nor have fun in the kitchen. There was only pain and darkness. All I could do was settle in my armchair

CHAPTER 1 • LET THERE BE LIGHT

as comfortably as possible and meditate. And so it was that I meditated for hours at a time, joining with the tall poplar tree outside my window, enjoying the beauty of nature, enfolded by the warm, loving, healing arms of the Source of Life.

Not accustomed to allopathic remedies, the recommended pain relief tablets made me feel dizzy, and the cream did nothing to alleviate the pain. The following day, a friend picked up some homeopathic granules and Bach Flower Remedies for me at the local health food store. I figured I'd address the dark funk as well as the physical problem. My work with the Bach Flower Remedies dated back half a century, so it was easy to pick out the ones I needed for my current situation. I started with my usual, basic personality type—Water Violet, for the quiet, monk-like isolator personality—and added Pine for self-appreciation and Larch for confidence in my ability to finish this book.

Remarkably, within a couple of days, the pain had subsided considerably. I let a few more days pass before making normal use of the arm, not wanting to aggravate the situation. My recovery was so rapid that some of my friends asked for help to select Bach Flower Remedies for them and their family members, something I was all too pleased to do. I even dusted off the Certificate from a course I had taken over 20 years ago and put it up on my wall.

During the following week, very slowly, I began organizing the notes for my book. Since I was still resting my arm, I worked with pen and paper while comfortably seated on my balcony. I also got help from my tech guy on how to deal with the computer problem temporarily. While my arm and shoulder continued to heal, Rock Water and Impatiens were added to my Bach Flower mix, addressing my need for flexibility and patience.

While perusing my notes from 2017, I came across an interesting entry. Although I do not recall the issue being addressed at the time—likely some channelled work recommended by a friend—I was surprised by its relevance and helpfulness. This is an example of the main reason I record the guidance as it comes to me; I tend to forget it. So I was very glad for my neurotic process of recording, dictating and printing, and, of course, multiple backups.

"If you are thinking of these things, you are thinking and not listening. So already, it is a distraction. You may also be thinking of things or placing your attention on things that are not appropriate or not needed by you. You were picking up on information that is currently being circulated. It is okay to let it go now. You will be shown what you need to see; you will be told what you need to know for your own growth.

"If you persist in this direction with these materials, if you get tangled up and caught up in it, you could be putting your attention in a direction that would actually delay your unfolding, pointing you in a direction that is not needed or is even inappropriate for you. Not all of the information that is currently circulating is appropriate for you. While you pursue these avenues, you will strengthen the imagery associated with the messages. You will maintain these pictures in your mind, again, very likely causing a distraction or delay in your own unfolding.

"Information can only be harmful if it causes fear, doubt, uncertainty, divisiveness, I'm right you're wrong, you're not following my path, hatred, etc. Only pursue these interests out of simple curiosity; do not let any of these images or ideas dwell in your mind, dwell in your awareness. They colour your view or your vision, and hinder your progress. As we have seen, your vision is growing increasingly clear. There is no need to push it or attempt to accelerate the process.

"There is nothing wrong with being aware of what is going on because you will have clients who are aware of these things and will ask questions of you. However, simply do not dwell on them. Be aware that all information is not appropriate for everyone at the same time. And yes, you are right in thinking that some of these messages may not be reflecting the truth. While you are thinking and perhaps adjusting your belief structures, you are not in a clear, open position to sense what is right and what is wrong, to sense the truth."

Yes, indeed. Needing to get back to my peaceful path, I turned to those teachings that brought me comfort—those that were anything but confusing and contradictory. In a moment of quiet contemplation, I heard—and felt—the loving words "welcome back." I breathed a deep sigh of relief. Yes, peace is so much better than confusion and darkness.

Meeting the True Self

Over the weeks that followed, the darkness faded, and I began to see very clearly, as though with fresh new eyes. Everything I had learned over a lifetime of study started to come together and make more sense than it ever had. The meaning of life was shifting. It became clear that as we transition into the Age of Aquarius, humanity is at a major crossroads—perhaps the most significant one we have encountered in a very long time—and we are in the driver's seat. It is time, now. As the weeks turned into months, my perspective continued to shift, but the book remained on the back burner. How could I write about what I saw in a way that would be easily understood, let alone accepted, by those who had never pursued a spiritual path—the ones I felt needed to be reached? How would those who were not familiar with or even remotely interested in astrology receive this work?

What might initially have appeared as resistance to writing turned out to be a vital timeout allowing for new learning to be discovered and appreciated while clearing out what was no longer relevant. Old, deeply buried beliefs about who and what I was, those beliefs that stood in the way of further progress, were released. As the vibrant colours of summer yielded to the golden hues of autumn, I swept away chunks of garbage from my tunnel, particularly the sticky doubts about my credentials as a writer that crept up from time to time. I wasn't a doctor; I wasn't a scientist or a pastor; I wasn't a channeller; I didn't have a Ph.D. or any other fancy degree. Plus, according to some, as an astrologer, I was performing the work of the devil. Garbage! All garbage. Out it all went. It was all garbage. I may not be a doctor or a scientist or a pastor, but I

AQUARIUS: THE AGE OF REVELATION, CHOICE AND TRANSFORMATION

Am. I Am, and You Are, and that is all that matters. We are Life expressed; therefore, each one of us has a voice, a voice that deserves and needs to be heard.

In December, just as I was getting back into the writing, my life was put on pause once again. This time, the flare-up was in my right arm, with pain that was worse than it had been back in May—if that were even possible. Being right-handed, as might be imagined, that put a stop to everything. I was stunned. Why had this happened again? What was I doing wrong? What more did I need to learn?

Very simply, this time around, I was reminded of a significant attribute of the human soul. Maybe I study and write about strange, spiritual, New Age, esoteric topics—at least to some, actually just about everyone I know—but there is one lesson that is not esoteric. It is a lesson that everyone has learned and, above all, experienced: that we are all capable of giving and receiving love. As friends stepped up to help with groceries or to help me put on my coat when I was ready to go for a walk or help retrieve the phone that had fallen behind my dresser, I knew that love surrounded me. And that is the greatest lesson of all, the perfect lesson for the Age of Aquarius. We are never alone, and love is in everyone and everything, even in a challenging health issue.

Interestingly, a post I had shared a couple of years earlier popped up as a memory on my social media page.

> *As humiliating as it may seem, when you ask for help, you provide an opportunity for a kind soul to make the gift of helping. So please ask, so someone can open their heart and discover all that they have to give. To ask is to make a great gift.*

Once again, I prepared some Bach Flower Remedies. This time I included Vervain—I tend to overwork once I get started—and Scleranthus to address the remaining ambivalence about writing.

CHAPTER 1 • LET THERE BE LIGHT

Again, the pain and inflammation went away remarkably quickly. In just over a week, I was able to flap my arm up and down like I was ready to fly. My friends were so impressed that once again, I was asked to help identify Remedies for friends and family members. It appears that this passing health issue was an invitation for me to share my knowledge of a wonderful healing aid I had left behind many years ago, something I was most pleased and honoured to do.

In the midst of turmoil or challenges of any kind, it is easy to forget that deep within us lies a wise inner voice. Everyone has heard it at least once in their lives—that voice of wisdom. It is the small voice deep inside, the mature one that knows what is right and keeps us from making mistakes. It is also known as the voice of the true Self and is different from the small self—or ego—which is nothing more than a limited version of who and what we are. The true Self is the actual driving force behind our life experiences, whether they are easy and joyful or challenging and even disheartening. Fortunately, the true Self never abandons its mission and it has the wisdom to use any circumstance or situation as an opportunity for learning, healing and growth. The true Self waits patiently for our invitation so it can step in and be the new director of our lives.

And so, after two weeks of timeout for healing and helping friends and family with Bach Flower Remedies, I reviewed and edited this chapter. Then I switched keyboards and treated myself to a bit of piano time. If you ask me, "I Could Write a Book" was the perfect song to learn.

CHAPTER 2

Doorway to a New Age

Even if you write a book and no one ever reads it besides you, that energy has been put down now on paper or is sitting in a computer, and it has an impact on the human collective consciousness. (*Ascension: The Shift to the Fifth Dimension*, Vol 2. p. 48)

You Raise Me Up

I hesitated before bringing up the subject of astrology in a book on awakening. In over fifty years in the field, I have encountered a few less-than-welcoming looks and comments. The raised eyebrows at business networking breakfasts and luncheons were understandable, if not a bit amusing, as were the surprised looks when I won a Chamber of Commerce Accolades award. I had grown accustomed, perhaps even immune to such responses. However, the abrupt termination of my numerology self-discovery series offered at no charge to teens in a local high school was disheartening, especially since the students were really enjoying it.

Perhaps a little more startling were the disparaging remarks about my profession from the so-called spiritually-minded, including *Course in Miracles* students. If you think about it, the fact that science has not yet provided an answer to the origins of life does not mean that we do not exist. Likewise, the fact that science has not yet proved that astrology and numerology can provide helpful information about the human experience does not mean that they do not. Okay, so I encountered another clump of garbage that needed to be thrown out. Taking a deep breath, I let it go.

AQUARIUS: THE AGE OF REVELATION, CHOICE AND TRANSFORMATION

But I understood. Each person has their filters and boundaries, which will apply to any topic, from baking to spirituality to science. I, too, have my boundaries, so some topics are too "out there" for me. I am a rather practical person, which is essential in my work with clients. Fortunately, as we shift into the Age of Aquarius, we are becoming increasingly aware of the profound and extensive relationship we have with each other, our planet and our universe. Boundaries on many levels are being brought to light, acknowledged and, as deemed necessary, laid aside.

Despite the hesitation, the subject kept coming to mind, more specifically, the transition from the Age of Pisces to the Age of Aquarius. I saw how a view of the human condition from this perspective could help shed light on the unsettled state of humanity on Earth at this time. It showed the interconnectedness of our past with the new climate ahead, underlining the importance of the choices we make today and the level of consciousness from which we make these choices. The transition phase between Eras is critical as adjustments must be made to make the best use of the potential of the new Era. It calls us to pause and seriously consider what we want but also who and what we are, for this will determine our future.

Just to get it out of my system, I wrote a three-part article for my blog, but, in the end, I didn't post it. The point was not to make predictions or stir up fear or concern. I wanted to use the Eras as a backdrop for another—albeit unique—way of looking at and understanding the human condition, a subject that would require a far more in-depth explanation than what a few short blog posts would allow. This may sound odd coming from a professional astrologer, but the truth is that the future is not predetermined; the future is a consequence of the choices made and the actions taken by the human collective given a particular climate. It is our choices that ultimately determine our future.

While the inner voice encouraged me to continue with this subject, reassuring me, as it has done so many times in the past, that I would have the help I needed along the way, still, I hesitated. Although I could go ahead with the writing and disregard what

CHAPTER 2 • DOORWAY TO A NEW AGE

others might say or think, there was another, deeper, more serious problem. I didn't like what I had seen for the future of humanity. It appeared dark, frightening and without hope, and, at the time, I didn't have any other way of seeing it. Every day I would go to my computer, open the documents I had started, stare at them a few minutes, then turn around and head to the kitchen to experiment with new recipes, or head to the other keyboard and do another piano lesson, or go shopping with my neighbour, or go for long walks or visit the ducks on the island near my condo. At least there were fun things to do.

What troubled me was a vision I'd had a couple of decades earlier, a gloomy image that I had managed to keep tucked away in the recesses of my mind until the pandemic of 2020. At that time, I had seen how in some distant future—hopefully not in my lifetime—the "problem" of overpopulation (as though living beings were a problem) could be addressed with the use of bio-weaponry. I then saw how, in the most inhumane way, the next step would be to replace labourers and workers with robots and AI-based technology. War was not likely to be an option, at least not the traditional kind of war known to man throughout history. The weapons now available to humans would more than likely lead to the annihilation of all life on the planet. From what I could see, the way ahead did not look promising.

Then, to add to the gloom, a few years ago, I woke up one night with the disturbing realization that as we transition from the Age of Pisces to the Age of Aquarius, we are actually moving backwards in the zodiac. This was indeed disconcerting since, from what I could see, short of a miraculous shift in consciousness, world events of recent years appeared to forewarn of a possible regressive trend for humanity, one that could be disastrous.

Then, of course, there were the dark, lingering images from the time I read George Orwell's powerful work, *1984*. Over fifty years later, there they were, stuck in my 12th house along with all the other garbage I had accumulated. Whether or not this was appropriate reading material for a young, unworldly, naive, spiritually-inclined sixteen-year-old is another matter. I have often wondered how the youth of today would react to this book. However, it was required reading for my grade 11 literature class, and so I set aside my Lobsang Rampa and astrology books and did as instructed. I read the book and poured my heart into the required essay.

That book struck me so hard that I felt like a zombie for weeks after having read it. According to my teacher, my essay was the best one I had ever written, and I was no literary scholar! My brain was attuned to math, not words. The subject of my essay was freedom— a vital attribute of the Age of Aquarius. And here we are now, in a time that may begin to resemble an Orwellian era, in which many may be wondering if their fundamental freedoms are being assailed through the misuse of invasive technological tools and political, economic and other control measures.

So what was I to do now? I wanted to write, I was ready to write, but I was stuck. In answer to my call, while exploring new works, I found the help I needed. I was shown a broader picture of the journey of humanity, of our story and of our potential, one that took us a whole step above the current human condition. While I listened to audiobooks and workshops, I felt my consciousness rise; at times, I felt as though I was being pulled up above my bodily form. There *is* a new way forward for humanity, a way that requires that we rise above the current level of consciousness.

Interestingly, in one of my beginner piano chords courses, I was introduced to a song I was not familiar with: "You Raise Me Up," composed by the Norwegian-Irish duo Secret Garden. I downloaded the version performed by Josh Groban just to get a feel for it. I find it easier to learn a song when I am familiar with it. In a matter of seconds, the song tore me apart. I cried and cried and cried for two days; every time I played the song, I cried. It brought to mind the help that is being extended to us—to all of humanity—as we struggle during this intense period of transition.

I became aware of the support that had been there throughout my life but that I had not fully recognized and not wholly let in. I sensed the presence of the awakened ones, the kind, gentle, loving, enlightened Beings that stand as guides and helpers as we reach up to be with them, where we belong. I dropped the ancient barriers and let in the help, the support and the love. I let myself be raised up, and I cried and cried and cried. To this day, I still can't listen to this song without shedding a tear or two—the Josh Groban version, that is, not my simple piano chords version—okay, maybe the hint of a tear.

After several months of study, following an evening meditation, I saw how to proceed with the writing. It came in a flash of insight that lifted my spirit so far above my old way of seeing that I found myself taking huge, deep breaths—so huge that I was surprised to discover how large my lungs were! In that moment of clarity, I saw how humanity is at a critical crossroads, but I also saw that we have the help we need to make the transition. If help is here, it means that many brothers and sisters on the planet have asked for help, and as seekers, we are not alone. It also means that we want change, and we are ready for change, which is an essential first step.

And so it is that the following morning, after a walk with my neighbour, and after making a mango mousse cake and after listening to a section in an audiobook—okay, after a few more hours of hesitation—I finally hit the keyboard, the computer keyboard this time.

The Shift from Pisces to Aquarius

If you are wondering what astrology has to do with *A Course in Miracles* or awakening or enlightenment or anything spiritual, not to worry; this isn't an astrology textbook, nor is prior knowledge of the subject required. The long-term cycles known as the Eras, or the Ages, will be examined with a focus on the last couple of Eras. Note that this is not an exhaustive work on the history of humanity; it serves simply as a means of gaining a perspective on the dynamics of the human journey. The transition period that occurs as one Era gives way to another can provide invaluable information on how to proceed by shedding light on where we have been, where we are now, and where we are going in the future. We are presently experiencing one such intersection, that is, between Pisces and Aquarius, and, as we will see, this is a particularly significant one.

What follows is a basic introduction to the Astrological Eras. Note that since throughout my childhood I was generally more curious about times to come rather than the present, let alone the past (no doubt an attribute of my forward-thinking Aquarius Moon), the study of history was not my strong suit. A few historical events have been selected for illustration purposes only, that is, to provide a sense of the climate of the Eras. As we shall see, the future is not set in stone, nor is it solely determined by an Era. Whether we like it or not, what we are now learning is that we are, in fact, far more responsible for the current—and future—condition of the world than we realize, or perhaps might even dare—or desire—to acknowledge.

While doing research for this section, I must admit that I came to a whole new appreciation for my youthful interest in the future and almost total lack of interest in the past. Even a brief study uncovers that the history of humanity on this planet leaves a lot to be desired. At the same time, our present condition shows a significant—even urgent—need for improvement. The study of history can be an important component in our learning because being familiar with past choices and actions can help us avoid making the same mistakes as we move forward into a new, uncharted Age. Not surprisingly, this little bit of research simply validated and further strengthened my awareness of the need for a significant shift in consciousness for humanity. In fact, what we really need is a consciousness revolution.

Some may recall "Aquarius/Let the Sunshine In" performed by The 5th Dimension, a pop song that reached number one on the U.S. Billboard chart in 1969. It heralded the coming of a golden age, a time of peace, love, harmony, vision and the freeing of the human mind—a radical New Age. At that time, the hippie movement was in full bloom, advocating communal living, harmony with nature, sharing resources, and creative self-expression. The

CHAPTER 2 · DOORWAY TO A NEW AGE

long trek through the Age of Pisces was coming to an end, and the bold new Age of Aquarius was emerging.

While striking a deep chord with many young people of the day, the idealistic message expressed in the song eventually faded and was replaced by the call to focus on the everyday practical realities of adult life. It is not uncommon for the youth of a generation to express new, even outrageous ideas for the world. But almost without fail, sometimes after having been told by an elder or a friend to be reasonable or more likely, to "grow up," they set aside their youthful idealism and turn their attention to job, family and financial security—essentially, primary survival concerns. Like the countless generations of youth before them, they join the ranks of the grown-up human adult, leaving behind seeds of potential growth and change.

While the Fifth Dimension were enjoying their musical success, I was deeply engaged in a search for the meaning of life. But while I too eventually engaged in a brave attempt to find my place in the world by trying various "normal" grown-up jobs, I never stopped searching for the truth—a quest that laid the foundation for a career as an astrologer-numerologist. In my early teens, I had read a book about Edgar Cayce and had been instantly intrigued by the idea that somehow it was possible to tap into the future and glimpse what was to come. Infected since childhood with a pervasive divine discontent that seemed to prevent me from finding joy in a relatively peaceful and abundant life, I wanted to know what the future held for me, more particularly, if it held the promise of true happiness.

Over the years that followed, I adopted the belief that the road ahead depended on choices and decisions we had made in the present. It seemed like a naïve belief at the time, but it helped me keep going in a world that consistently failed to make sense on the deep level with which I was concerned. I think I actually believed that, to a certain extent, we did create our future, though I did not understand why it was so difficult to successfully create a future that was filled with lasting peace and joy. Eventually, I concluded that my desire for peace in a world of increasing noise and chaos appeared to be little more than a pie-in-the-sky dream. Looking back now, I realize that my vision was fifty years ahead of its time.

Half a century later, with that pileup of planets in Capricorn about to move into the first house of my astrology chart, I finally sensed the promise of a new beginning for humanity just around the corner as Jupiter, Saturn and eventually, Pluto, would move into Aquarius. The time had come. Whatever the trigger, I couldn't help but be curious about how humankind would fare during this significant transition into the most interesting Age of Aquarius. Knowledge of astrology is not needed to realize that change is needed, and the time for this change is now.

Since the advent of the industrial revolution in the late 18th century, and more so over the last fifty years, we have experienced incredible growth in the fields of medicine, technology, agriculture, manufacturing, transportation, communications and science. Yet, while we send vehicles out in space, many of our brothers and sisters—far too many, in fact, one is too many—continue to subsist in extreme poverty without access to the basic necessities of life, without healthy food, shelter and proper medical care. While grocery stores throw away millions of tons of food every year, 8 million people die of starvation every year. We live in a world of undeniable social, cultural and economic inequality where a person's worth continues to be measured by material wealth and power. We are guests on a beautiful planet for which we have no respect, behaving as though we are superior beings—some more superior than others—with the right to do as we please.

As though in answer to my prayer for a hopeful outcome, it occurred to me that while this transition from Pisces to Aquarius might not be easy, the fact that we are moving into a less complex climate might be a good thing. Those who are even a little bit familiar with astrology are aware of how completely different Pisces and Aquarius are from each other. While it may appear that we are moving backwards from Pisces to Aquarius, it is as though we are caught in a vise-grip that is tightened to the max. The pressure is on, and the call is impossible to ignore. As difficult as this may seem, this is a good thing. It's hard to remain asleep once the fire alarm has been triggered. We now have the opportunity to make significant changes for humanity—the keyword being *now*.

A global shift in consciousness is indeed afoot—a much-needed shift—a cry from humanity for a new way, for a far better way for all life on this planet. But how will it unfold? It is naïve to think that simply moving into a new era—a "Golden Age"—will bring the good, the peace and the light we desire. No matter how enlightened or "golden" this promised New Age may appear, we will first need to unload the garbage we have collected during the last couple of Eras. We will also need to trust that ridding ourselves of our surplus baggage will not leave us feeling bereft; that, instead, our needs will be met; and that, on the contrary, more will come into our experience.

How will we move forward in a new climate that seems more confusing than ever? Are we ready to let go of the old and embrace the new? How much of the old are we willing to release? How much new are we willing to embrace? Or, will we continue down the same old beaten path travelled by our ancestors, only now, with fancier technology? Do we have it in our hearts to bring about and embrace this much-needed change with grace, harmony and wisdom?

An Overview of the Eras

When exactly will this shift happen? The Eras can be likened to seasons. There is no exact time when, for example, winter ends and spring begins; some transitions from one season to another are quick, while others are slow. So there is no precise date for the end of one Era and the start of another, nor will the shift happen overnight. Where I live in Canada, when we are transitioning between seasons, we never know how to dress. When we shift from winter to spring, we can have a couple of warm spring days followed by the occasional cold, snowy day. One day we pull out sandals and shorts, the next day, it's back to boots, mitts and winter coats. Similarly, as we shift from Pisces to Aquarius, we will encounter a mix of both climates, which may explain the seeming uncertainty and confusion, the lack of harmony and coherence experienced by humanity on the planet at this time.

The Eras are periods of roughly 2100 years based on the division of the Great Year into 12. The Great Year is a cycle of approximately 26,000 years determined by the precession of the equinoxes—the trajectory traced by the polar axis of the Earth. Just as with the change in seasons, there is a transition phase of a couple of hundred years between Eras as life on Earth adjusts to the new climate. This point suggests that we have a role to play in the unfolding of the new Era, something we will need to consider more closely.

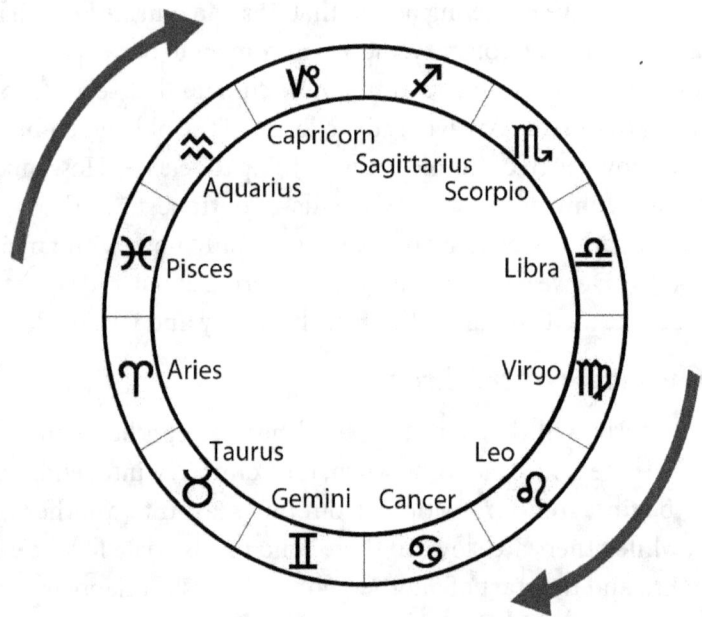

The nature of an Era is portrayed by the characteristics of one of the 12 signs of the zodiac. Each sign has the attributes of one of the four elements: fire, earth, air or water, as well as those of one of the three crosses, or quadruplicities, cardinal, fixed or mutable. The fire and air elements represent masculine or yang energies, while the earth and water elements represent feminine or yin energies. Each sign also has a planet—or ruler—with which it has a close affinity.

CHAPTER 2 • DOORWAY TO A NEW AGE

We are now leaving a period of approximately 2000 years during which the attributes, or climate, of the mutable water sign Pisces were in place. Pisces is associated with the planet Neptune. The mutable quality of the sign makes it multi-faceted, sociable, dualistic, flexible, adaptable, hierarchical and relational. The water element of the sign makes it creative, receptive, sensitive, changeable and capable of experiencing a wide range of emotions.

Pisces is associated with beliefs, rationalization and reasoning, the development of rules and regulations, systems of government, community, business, information and education, as well as the establishment of social, cultural and religious institutions and hierarchies. Caring and sensitive by nature, Pisces natives can develop a strong sense of responsibility and obligation for others and are often found in health care and other support functions. Given their very generous nature, they can, at times, take on more than their fair share.

On the traditional wheel of the zodiac, the signs progress with increasing complexity from Aries to Pisces, with Pisces being the most complex of the 12 signs. Just think of the popularity of tragedy, romance and mystery as literary genres or high-intensity drama in popular movies and literature. The Pisces Era also inspired the extraordinary creations of classical composers and artists such as Beethoven, Mozart, Chopin, Brahms, van Gogh, da Vinci and Monet. As the final expression of the zodiac, Pisces holds an ocean of infinite possibilities.

Aquarius is a fixed air sign and is associated with the planet Uranus. I should mention a slight misunderstanding about the nature of Aquarius, also known as the water bearer (Verseau in French). This is likely due to the fact that when the ancients assigned attributes to the signs, the concept of energy had not yet been discovered. I saw Aquarius more as an "energy" bearer, certainly not a "water" bearer. Given the growing interest in vibration, frequency, energy, consciousness, mind and awareness by a growing number of scientists and researchers as well as spiritual teachers, a more accurate designation for Aquarius in these times might be the "consciousness" bearer.

The air element of Aquarius is expressed as great intellectual curiosity, while the fixed quality of the sign makes it a tangible, even practical curiosity. Aquarius is known to be progressive, inventive, modern and forward-thinking, and is quite open to, and can actually derive a certain satisfaction from, revolutionary thinking. Fiercely independent, natives of this sign will seek the freedom to follow their deep, usually unique, aspirations and are apt to experience life unbound by the rules of tradition. They prefer the beat of their own drum rather than that followed by the crowd. Progressive-minded and naturally inquisitive, they tend to push the envelope and may find themselves to be running ahead of their time. They are often more comfortable "outside the box." However, as contradictory as this may seem, whatever they get involved in must have some practical relevance. Contrary to Pisces, which is faith- or belief-based, Aquarius is science-minded and fact-based.

Yet, despite an affinity for science and cold, hard logic, Aquarians are humanitarian at heart. They hold a strong sense of community and recognize the need for more equality in the world. They can also express great intuition and creativity, indicating that they may be more in tune with pure Source or higher consciousness than they realize. Interestingly, over the past few decades, science has made great strides in the study of consciousness—a subject once reserved for adepts of parapsychology, esoterics, spirituality and metaphysics. These fascinating new studies can be found in the works of Gregg Braden, Bruce Lipton and the Global Consciousness Project.

Note that every chart contains the 12 zodiac signs, and so everyone has access to the energies available in each sign regardless of whether or not they have the Sun or any other planet in that sign. Also, because a person has a planet in a sign does not guarantee that this energy will be used in an enlightened manner. The positions of the planets in a chart indicate areas of focus, unique skills and abilities, and opportunities for healing, learning and growth. So, even if a chart contains no planets in Aquarius, as it is

CHAPTER 2 · DOORWAY TO A NEW AGE

an integral part of the zodiacal matrix, its qualities and attributes remain always available.

The history buff may be curious to explore the human journey in earlier Eras. Going back two Ages before Pisces, approximately 4200–2100 BC, we have the period known as the Bronze Age. It was aligned with Taurus, a fixed earth sign associated with the planet Venus, known in ancient times as the goddess of love, desire, fertility and prosperity. It covers the period when the hunter-gatherer nomadic tribes of the previous Gemini Era (a mutable air sign) settled the lands, giving birth to agriculture, food reserves, baking, construction, home-building, towns, architecture and mining. During the Age of Taurus, planetary positions were used to identify the best times for planting and harvesting crops. Taurus is the sign associated with all things physical, from the physical body and the sensory experience to all forms of material acquisition, wealth, assets and banking. It is the sign of worth and value. It was during this period that the first pyramids were built, and the memory of departed souls was honoured with the process of mummification.

The Age of Taurus was followed by the Age of Aries, approximately 2100–0 BC. Aries is a cardinal fire sign and is associated with the planet Mars, known as the god of war. This period saw the rise of the affirmation of the individual as distinct from the whole, even ready to fight for a place in the world; the development of mathematics and number systems, enterprise, criminal laws, shipbuilding, trade and the Iron Age. Authoritarian and potentially aggressive, Aries can foster a competitive warrior mentality, hence the domination of the world populations by militaristic empires during this period. This Era saw the birth of the Olympics.

Taurus is a yin/feminine sign. So, it is not surprising that during the Age of Taurus, the matriarchy or the feminine principle held a significant position in the culture. Being a yang/masculine sign, Aries fostered a patriarchal society and the introduction of God the "Father," an all-powerful male deity. Since Pisces is a yin/feminine sign, one can't help but wonder how humanity would have fared under female leadership over the past 2000 years. Aquarius is a yang/masculine sign, but it can be considered nearly gender-neutral given its inclination to disregard or blur boundaries. In this context, the current demand for gender equality and a sense of gender confusion arising among many young souls today makes sense.

The transition from one Era to another is not a simple matter of turning the page and starting at zero. Life is like school. What was learned in first grade is further developed and expanded in second grade, etc. Humans have been living and learning on planet Earth for thousands of years, and so what has been learned and gathered in previous Eras is brought forward into the new Era—the good along with the bad. Each Era is thus founded on the collective learning and experiences gathered over eons of time.

When zooming in on the last few Eras, we see what lessons have been brought forward. During the Age of Taurus, identification with the body and all things material was reinforced and valued. While the desire to acquire and accumulate goods grew, so did our dependency on these goods. In time, worth was determined by the amount of goods acquired. During the Age of Aries, we learned to be self-reliant and go after what we desired—ready and willing to fight for what we wanted, if necessary. Over the past 2000 years, standards, belief systems, regulations, norms and rules—all attributes of Pisces—were put into place as a means of establishing controls and managing the whole while humanity continued to experience growth and expansion.

As we shift from Pisces to Aquarius, we are moving from a complex, multilayered, hierarchical climate that thrives on emotion, reasoning, justification and beliefs to a climate with a low tolerance for emotion-fuelled behaviour, a climate based on logic, science and first-hand experience rather than on blind faith. While a large number of the human collective learned to yield authority to those higher on the ladder of social-economic power during the past three Eras, this is likely to change in Aquarius. The consciousness pioneer of this new Era is not as likely to follow the commands of those in power. Because this new climate is so different from the previous ones, we have the opportunity to make significant changes for

CHAPTER 2 · DOORWAY TO A NEW AGE

humanity, but always—and this is the crucial point—if this is what we choose. Fortunately, as we move forward into this new Era, we are beginning to see evidence of change as a growing number of individuals are standing up for their worth, as well as that of all of humanity and the planet.

What makes this period particularly interesting from the astrological perspective is the concentration of outer planets traversing the same quadrant of the sky. During the 18 years from 2008 to 2026, Jupiter, Saturn and Neptune will have travelled from Capricorn to Pisces, with a focus on Aquarius right in the middle of these two signs. Pluto will spend most of that time in Capricorn, beginning its transit in Aquarius in 2023. It's almost as though the universe is saying: "Look over here. Look at the old patterns you have established over the past thousands of years." This would be in keeping with the nature of Capricorn, which is associated with all things ancient, old and traditional. These transits are pointing out that perhaps some of the old needs to be released before we can move forward and explore the new. There is a call to take stock of what can be made better, what can be healed, what can be released so we can have a more enlightened experience in the Age of Aquarius.

♑ Capricorn	♒ Aquarius	♓ Pisces
Jupiter 2019–2020	Jupiter 2020–2021	Jupiter 2021–2022
Saturn 2017–2020	Saturn 2020–2023	Saturn 2023–2025
Pluto 2008–2024	Pluto 2024–2044	Neptune 2011–2025

The table above is a rough layout of the transits of Jupiter, Saturn, Neptune and Pluto between 2008–2026. Due to retrograde motion, or the apparent backward movement as viewed from the geocentric perspective, a planet will not necessarily shift to the following sign in one day. For example, Pluto's shift into Aquarius will go back and forth between March 2023 and November 2024. Note that this is less about precise celestial geometry and more about the overall theme, as it shows what I saw as a window of opportunity from my perspective as an astrologer. Following this brief moment in time, the journey of humanity on planet Earth will continue. The question remains: Will we continue as before? Or will we have made the needed changes?

In the broader timeframe of the Eras, this represents a very narrow window; in fact, it is nothing but a tiny blip on the timeline of humanity. Maybe this passing series of transits is but a nanosecond in humanity's long journey, but it can be welcomed as a powerful opening, an opportunity like none other to experience a significant shift in consciousness, one that will take humanity out of the restrictive perspectives of our sleep state into fully awakened consciousness.

While the transition from one Era to another can take a couple of hundred years, given the emergence of New Thought and New Age movements and the rapid progress of science and technology over the past 200 years, we can see that the transition into the Age of Aquarius is well underway. On December 21, 2020, we witnessed the Jupiter-Saturn conjunction in Aquarius, the first in this sign since the 1400s. If there is one significant marker in time indicating our first steps into the Age of Aquarius, this Jupiter-Saturn conjunction would be it. As intense as it may seem from the human perspective, this period is clearly the doorway to a New Age for humanity.

Embracing the Shift

Regardless of whether or not you are open to information gleaned from celestial cycles, know that it is not the Era that determines the quality of life for humanity; it only sets the stage for a climate, offering up possibilities. As I tell my clients, just because it is winter and there is snow on the ground does not mean that you will automatically become a championship skier or even take up the sport. You may prefer to stay home and learn to play the blues harp. Then again, if you go out in the snow barefoot wearing shorts, you may find the season most uncomfortable, even disagreeable. The point is to make choices that are appropriate for the season and your unique learning and life needs.

While it is possible to recognize an Era by its intrinsic zodiacal qualities, how this transition unfolds will depend on the decisions we make, actions taken in response to the calls of humanity for change, for fairness for all of our brothers and sisters around the globe. The Eras do not determine our lives; we do. The foundation of our future is determined here and now by our choices.

The future we create for our children and grandchildren will be the result of all that has gone before combined with the decisions and actions we take today. In the coming months and years, if we attempt to rebuild our world with old, outdated structures, we will likely encounter significant obstacles and possibly be faced with other crises. It would be like heading into the spring season with the tools used in winter. Would you expect to easily and successfully plant seedlings in the garden with a snowplow?

The shift will occur to the degree that we allow it. It will not be forced or imposed upon us. The transition will be smooth and comfortable if we flow with it, or it will be uncomfortable and difficult if we resist it. Our experience will be determined by our openness to let in the new, our willingness to release the old, and our readiness to grow and expand with the movement. Remember always that we cannot build a new house with old materials. Sure, an old house can be renovated. But is that what we want? Do we want to paint things over, hold on to the past and pretend that everything is okay, or do we want to explore the possibility of creating a world for humanity that is completely different, one that meets the needs of all living beings, one that respects this beautiful planet, one that allows each person to rise to their ultimate expression? We have the opportunity and the potential now to break free of the past and to rise above previous limitations. Forget normal; how about entirely new?

There is no doubt that we are at a crossroads, and the time for change is now. For, how many Eras must we traverse before we understand and accept that Love is the only way? How many lifetimes must we engage in and discard before we come to the essential and crucial realization that we are all—each and every one of us—members of one family, the family of humankind? How much pain and misery must we suffer and endure and impose on each other before we finally accept that our Source/Creator is Love, that It has never stopped loving us, that It simply waits until we shake ourselves out of our sleeping stupor and accept that this Love is our natural inheritance?

CHAPTER 3

Breaking the Cycle

No belief is neutral. Every one has the power to dictate each decision you make. For a decision is a conclusion based on everything that you believe. (ACIM, Ch. 24, p. 554)

Teachings, Religion and Spirituality

During the transition into the New Age, teachings, beliefs, religions and cultural traditions which we have built, sustained, accepted and even fought and killed over for millennia will need to be re-evaluated since they are at the foundation of our current level of consciousness. In order to build a new world, a new foundation must also be created. The degree to which we are willing to accept and proceed with this shift into a higher level of consciousness will depend on our willingness to question every belief, every value that we hold. As we identify those beliefs that are no longer suitable, we will need to muster up the courage to either correct or altogether abandon them.

Since we are moving into a new Era, which, from our current perspective, appears as unknown territory, we must trust that something better can and will take the place of what we have known for so long. And so it is that as the shift unfolds, corrections are being made to traditional teachings, ancient teachings are being brought to light, and new teachings are emerging. With this abundance of help, a new way of seeing and knowing ourselves is opening up for humanity.

Wisdom or spiritual teachings have been around for as long as humanity has been in need of them, which is very likely for as long as humanity has existed here on Earth. Some have been gathered through inspiration or insight by souls who were in touch with their "higher Self." Other teachings have been channelled or transmitted to receptive souls by beings that hold a more enlightened perspective and are not bound by the confines of the human condition.

Teachings have been passed down through the ages in a variety of ways, from oral transmission to the written word. While some may consider oral transmission outdated, just think of those priceless words a wise parent or grandparent may have shared with you when you were young. Many teachings are handed down through family, community or cultural traditions. Most people do not fully realize that we teach all the time in subtle and sometimes less subtle ways, not only by our words but also by our thoughts, actions, attitudes and behaviour.

Some teachings have been tailored and organized in various ways to form schools of thought and religions. The content is then imparted to its adherents through lessons, systems of practice, ceremony and rituals. When transformed into written works, they tend to acquire a position of power and authority. In the face of authority, whether in written form or embodied in personality or status, many followers will abandon their ability to discern for themselves what is or is not appropriate for them at a given time. Although many of these teachings may have been founded on inspired messages and information based on truth, most are man-made structures, and many have strayed from the original messages on which they were based.

Numerous alterations, edits, interpretations, adaptations, omissions, additions, translations and changes have been made to ancient wisdom teachings over the centuries, oftentimes resulting in distortions of the original message. Some of these distortions were the result of simple misunderstanding or loss of clarity over time. Other distortions and corruptions were intentionally inserted by those who desired to misinform and take advantage of the population through the use of fear and other control measures. While there is truth at the root of all valid teachings, these distortions may prevent the core message from being fully conveyed. There is also the fact that while a teaching may have been relevant at the time it was received, since consciousness is constantly shifting, it may no longer be relevant today. Unless one is a seasoned religious scholar or an experienced historian, it may be difficult to sort through the alterations and ferret out the truth set forth in the original teachings.

Spirituality refers to the study of spirit, or soul, or that which is beyond the familiar 3-D/body/mind level of experience. Wisdom is the knowing that emerges when the mind is connected to the Source of Truth. Many new teachings are emerging today as more and more souls are reaching out in search of knowledge beyond the customary, traditional teachings with which we are familiar. This shows that when a call is made, it is answered, further indicating that something or someone "out there" can hear and even answer our calls. So much for our long-held—and now fading—belief that we are the only living beings in the universe.

It can be said that religion and spirituality are not necessarily the same thing. A person can engage in and adhere to religious practices without being spiritual, while another can be spiritual or spiritually-minded, without belonging to a church or religion or adhering to strict dogma. True spirituality serves to raise consciousness above the lower body/mind levels—to the levels of spirit, vibration, soul, energy, love, knowing and Mind. It is not defined nor bound by culture, traditions, merit, ritual, achievement, ceremony, structured beliefs or obedience to rules, laws, regulations or a master. Spirituality is effectively a quest for a direct experience of the Source of Life, a knowing of the true Self as an expression of Source Energy or God.

A Celestial Overview of Belief Systems

Whether one is engaged or even interested in wisdom or spiritual teachings, it is becoming increasingly apparent that humanity—or the human collective—has entered a significant transition period. This shift is global and profound, and it is infusing all levels of knowledge and awareness of self, the world and all of creation. We must find a way to get through this period of shift with as little turbulence, pain, disruption and struggle as possible because, by all appearances, this may not be an easy transition. How can we take advantage of this critical time to make the greatest leap forward for all of humankind?

One way is to examine the origins of our beliefs since they reflect the level of consciousness we held when they were adopted. Until we experience higher levels of consciousness, our beliefs will continue to colour and determine our thoughts and actions, hence the quality of life for us as individuals and for the collective. When accepted without question, beliefs can anchor us in the past or outdated, no longer relevant structures, delaying and even preventing any forward movement. Without a break from the past, it may be difficult to move forward with the freedom and openness needed for a full experience of the potential that lies ahead. Beliefs are like the stage on which the play of life is acted out. Do we have the right stage for the next act?

The transition between the past two Eras (Aries and Pisces) provides an interesting perspective on the evolution and development of the teachings, religions and belief systems that we have gathered and now carry with us as we stand at the doorway of the next Era. It also highlights the importance of paying attention to the present time since it is the choices we have made in the past that have determined the quality of life for humanity today. That being the case, it follows that the choices we make today will determine the quality of life for the coming years.

Due to the apparent backward trajectory of the precession of the equinoxes through the zodiac, it is as though over a 26,000 year period, we begin at the top of a ladder in Pisces and then step down through the twelve signs, or rungs, to Aries. Once complete, we begin again at the top of a new ladder and step back down. The shift from Aries to Pisces, which occurred about 2000 years ago, is therefore highly significant as it was a leap from the bottom rung of one ladder in Aries, the least complex sign, to the top rung of a new ladder in Pisces, the most complex sign.

This downward trajectory is in alignment with many of the teachings that are emerging today. These are revealing that we began our human journey as highly enlightened beings, fully aware of our wholeness, capable of experiencing many dimensions, conscious of ourselves as beings of energy, mind, spirit and love. Over thousands of lifetimes in the physical human form, we gradually became distracted by and entrenched in the dense, lower third dimension. Basically, we have lost all memory and any sense of our origins as divine, light/energy beings.

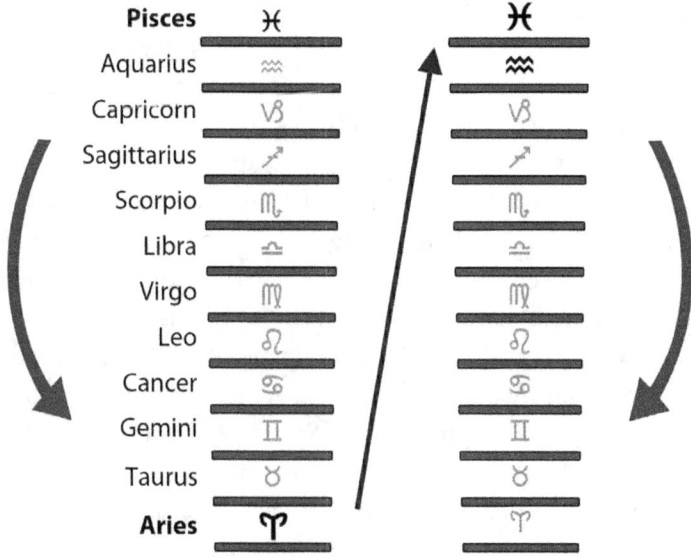

The Age of Aries presented mankind with a climate that was supportive of great energy and drive, a tremendous opportunity for action, industry, enterprise and exploration. During that time, the gods and goddesses of the previous Era of Taurus were brought together under one God, the Father/Mother/Source of all life, for the purpose of uniting humanity. In so doing, humans could then work together and build a world that met the needs of all. However, this period also held the less enlightened or lower consciousness ego-based Aries potential for war, conflict, confrontation, aggression, dominance, competition—an "us versus them" and an "I want what I want, and I want it now" attitude.

Once the aggressive and competitive option was selected, a warring god was chosen as an idol for the religions as well as the foundation of the beliefs of the time. A male-dominated (Aries/yang/fire) authority and rule-of-law were implemented, replacing the feminine climate (Taurus/yin/earth) of the previous Era. This was accomplished at times aggressively and with the use of violence, at the cost of many lives as commanded by those who had claimed authority. According to the laws of the time, all manner of killing, torture, murder, slavery, rape, war and pillaging were acceptable if carried out in the name of the established authority or idolized god.

Given the less than glorious choices made by mankind during that Era, the shift to the Age of Pisces provided humanity with an excellent opportunity to make a giant leap as we now moved onto an entirely new ladder. This shift of Eras was the perfect opportunity for bringing radical change and, above all, much-needed healing—a wonderful Pisces attribute—to the human condition. As the last and most complex sign, Pisces holds the potential for the highest experience of consciousness available to humanity, lifting the veil of ignorance and revealing our true spiritual nature and function as unique expressions of Source. This was embodied in the life work of Jesus, or Jeshua ben Joseph, as he was known at the time, in which he presented humanity with a simple, and yet most powerful message: that God, Father/Mother or Creator/Source is Love and to know God is to be Love. Since God is in all things, to love all is to know God.

This new teaching replaced the long-familiar authoritarian, warring god with a loving, non-judgmental God, a universal God whose love is bestowed on all of creation. Jesus exemplified our unlimited potential as expressions of Source Energy through forgiveness, healings and the willingness to see the Divine in all beings and in all things. By his resurrection, he swept aside the fear of death and

CHAPTER 3 · BREAKING THE CYCLE

the belief that we are mere bodies and instead demonstrated the invulnerability and infinite nature of a life aligned with truth.

These radical ideas were not an easy sell given the low level of consciousness held by the human collective at the time. In fact, they were basically contrary to the long-held familiar norm. What Jesus taught directly addressed the need to abandon violence, competition, aggression, hierarchies, domination, selfishness, war, division, slavery and greed, and to embrace love for all. He taught that all were equally worthy of the love of God. It is no surprise that his presence drew so much attention from the people, especially the many who had suffered loss, injustice, condemnation or illness. By the same token, it is not surprising that he was perceived as a threat to the established order and thereby so quickly silenced.

Clearly, the revolutionary changes in behaviour, attitudes, beliefs and life choices required by these new teachings were more than what could be welcomed, let alone accepted, at the time. Rather than choosing the potential for higher consciousness presented to us by Jeshua, humanity opted for the lower levels of manifestation of the Pisces Era. This choice for the lower option did not require significant changes in consciousness. With only minor modifications, it allowed for the preservation of the deeply entrenched structures, beliefs, dogmas, rules and laws accumulated over from the previous Eras. So it is that humanity carried its ancient baggage from the old ladder onto the new ladder.

During the transition from the Era of Aries to Pisces, self-deprecating teachings of sin, suffering, sacrifice and guilt, along with complex hierarchical systems and control measures, were put into practice. These measures were easy to implement since the low level of consciousness expressed during the two previous Eras—Aries and Taurus—supported self-focused, fear-based survivalist behaviour. The depreciation and control of the disempowered self through the use of guilt and fear of punishment was thus easy to implement as it had become a well-known, natural aspect of being human. The authoritative warring god of Aries was now changed into a judging, selective, punishing, divisive and cruel god. It was only natural that fear would be augmented as a prime motivator.

At its lowest level of expression, Pisces (in association with the planet Neptune) manifests as guilt, escapism, illusion, fantasy, divisiveness, inequality, deception, corruption, suffering, sacrifice, drama and addiction, common themes found in modern-day movies, television series and novels. Adding to these themes the anger, competitiveness, vengefulness and aggressiveness of Aries and the possessiveness, acquisitiveness, materialism and selfishness of Taurus, all lowest expressions of these Eras, we find the fodder for what we accept and choose as modern-day entertainment: best-selling novels, blockbuster movies, television series, sports and gaming industries. More importantly—and horrifyingly so—these are the themes underlying much of what has emerged over the last 2000 years for humanity and the planet.

It is true that some of the lower consciousness distortions and teachings of past Eras have been removed and replaced by more enlightened teachings, especially since the early 1800s. In each Era, works that serve to correct the misunderstandings of previous ages are introduced. For example, during the Aries Era, the many gods of Taurus, especially low-energy gods that inappropriately glorified the body and material possessions over mind and spirit, were replaced by one universal God. This correction reflected the concept of Oneness found in traditional Hinduism and Buddhism. However, the idea of a God of Oneness was not easy to accept in the competitive, enterprising climate of Aries, and a more exciting warring god was chosen instead. During Pisces, we were given the opportunity to replace the god of war with a God of love, a God with whom we could have a direct relationship. Here again, we were free to choose to accept or reject this teaching.

Many representatives—teachers, pastors, ministers, priests—of various faiths are making corrections and modifications to their respective teachings. Some may ultimately conclude that certain religions and thought systems are not designed to support what lies beyond the current human condition, as they were built to hold us within a limited frame of reference. While some religions will be abandoned, many will find commonality with others, for truth is true, no matter the language or culture or teaching. As community spirit is an intrinsic trait of Aquarius, it will be interesting to watch as those who were once on opposite sides of a fence will choose to remove all fences and work together.

The following brief look at the Eras, though certainly not exhaustive, may help us better prepare for the way forward as we move into the new Era of Aquarius. Keeping in mind that we carry forward old teachings and beliefs, if these are placed in the context of the climate of the new Era, it may be easier to release those which are outdated and no longer suitable. It is not necessary to dwell on the past. All that is needed is that we identify what is relevant for today and separate out what is not, thus preparing the way for change. We can then determine appropriate measures to bring about the desired change and, above all, a more enlightened experience for all of humanity. Are we ready to experience our full potential as direct expressions of an infinite, loving Source? Our choices will determine what we will experience.

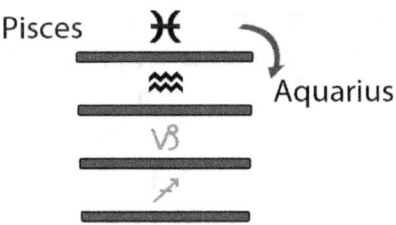

The Next Rung on the Ladder

As we step down the ladder from Pisces to the next rung into the Era of Aquarius, we once again find ourselves in a position of choice. But, we ask, what does an Aquarius climate look like? What kind of choices do we have? Will we like this new climate? Will we continue to have the freedom to do as we please? Can we have more freedom? What if we are not equipped for such a drastic change? What if we don't know how to make this transition? But here are the crucial questions: Are we ready for something different for ourselves and humanity? If we have a choice in the matter, what level of consciousness will we choose? How much of the old are we ready to release? How much change do we really want?

If there is one factor that can ignite a spark of curiosity and perhaps even a desire to explore a radical shift of consciousness, it is the very idea of freedom of choice. Aquarius thrives on and, more importantly, requires freedom. Another wonderful attribute of Aquarius is its innate curiosity and readiness to explore beyond the boundaries of the known. Since the human journey is now showing signs of expansion into a quest for freedom from the current limitations of the human condition, this new Era may very well provide the perfect climate for such advancement.

At the start of the Age of Aquarius, we have accumulated beliefs, teachings, customs, dogmas, rules, laws and practices from many Eras that clearly need to be re-evaluated. While life on Earth may appear to have improved for many over the past several hundred years, we must ask ourselves if these improvements represent all that we are capable of and all that we deserve. We have made gods out of matter; we base our worth on the acquisition of wealth and valuables; we have given ourselves permission to compete, cheat, steal and even kill for these possessions through our warring cultures. We have set aside any regard for the planet in our desire to manufacture and produce countless products, many of which are of questionable value, in order to grab a slice of the competitive economic world market. There is still tremendous inequality on the planet. With the use of fear, we have established complex hierarchies that justify the suffering, punishment and even slavery of many, while others rule and live in extreme, unnecessary, even obscene wealth and comfort.

We have built a world where factory workers who live in less affluent countries are basically slaves, sacrificing themselves (Pisces) so that companies can use cheap labour to manufacture goods, outdo the competition (Aries), sell more goods and make more money (Taurus). Although they may not see it this way since they claim freedom of lifestyle, office workers in affluent countries are themselves slaves to their jobs, motivated by fear of lack, addicted to their comfortable lifestyles, subject to beliefs and views as separate, seemingly independent selves, bodies in a world of form and matter. Most do not even question our less-than-enlightened cultural, economic, industrial, political and business practices, choosing instead to adhere to the familiar norm. Clearly, the deeper, higher consciousness Pisces teachings of our infinite potential and innate connection to a loving, fair, all-inclusive Life Principal/God has not quite reached our inner radar.

The climate of Aquarius differs very much from that of the last couple of Eras in that it favours fact- or science-based knowledge and information rather than faith-based teachings and religions. Aquarius is about cold hard facts rather than unsubstantiated beliefs. Given our track record with religions and belief systems that are not based on science or that cannot be validated in a tangible manner—meaning, with the tools of the day—it is understandable that a trend toward atheism and agnosticism, or "nones," as some non-believers are now being called, and the outright rejection of religion in favour of science has begun to emerge. Interestingly, a large percentage of "non-believers" believe in a "higher power."

A growing number of individuals are putting their trust and faith—even blindly so—in the science of the day. We are all aware that not so long ago, it was believed that the Earth was flat, that the sun and the planets revolved around the Earth and that we evolved from apes. The fact remains that science is not infallible, and it too is constantly in a state of development, growth and evolution. While what goes on in the lab or the R&D department may be creative, it is perhaps wise to keep in mind that most technological, pharmaceutical and scientific research is funded by commercial and business interests.

Research and studies in science, technology and industry can be fascinating for the inquisitive, even creative researcher—which are typical Aquarian traits. My years of work as a tech writer for an R&D consulting firm were more like play than work. While the exploration of new tools, techniques and technologies may be a captivating pursuit, when carried out by humans, who are, for the most part, still in a lower state of consciousness, the resulting outcome may not always be suitable for humankind or the planet. This is one of the flaws of scientific and technological development today.

Although this is slowly beginning to change, there is still a significant lack of concern for the planet when it comes to product development and consumerism. With built-in obsolescence and unacceptably short product lifespans—all of which serves to boost shareholder profits—our beautiful planet is becoming a massive dumping ground for discarded, outdated and "replaced-by-a-fancier-model" products. Most young people today are under the impression that an acceptable lifespan for an appliance is six or seven years, whereas not so long ago, appliances were designed to last at least 25 to 30 years, sometimes longer. It is doubtful that there is one grandma on the planet that would find this acceptable.

At its lowest level of manifestation, Aquarius can foster behaviour that is narrow-minded, arrogant, overconfident, dictatorial, rebellious, unyielding, cold, even heartless and inhumane, hence the frightening Orwellian view of the future of humanity that ignited my sense of urgency for a consciousness revolution. Without a major shift in consciousness, the kind, inclusive, humanitarian, inquisitive, equitable, open-minded, intelligent, solution-based attributes of Aquarius, which represent its higher expression, may be overlooked and perhaps even outright rejected in favour of its lower attributes. Where's the proof, they'll demand. Why should I believe that we are expressions of a loving God/Source when I can't see it?

As consciousness shifts, knowing will align with higher wisdom. For example, a scientist might reconsider proceeding with a research project if, given his greater awareness, he sees that humanity might not be ready for the resulting product. In this way, the development of atomic energy might have been postponed for another time, when it could be used more wisely, without the danger of being

CHAPTER 3 · BREAKING THE CYCLE

weaponized or causing harm to the planet. Similarly, while working on the development of a drug, a chemist might set aside her research simply based on a clear and strongly inspired hunch—a highly unscientific criterion for making a scientific decision. In this way, a product such as thalidomide might not have been sent to market and thousands of children would not have died at birth, or for those who survived, done so with severe health issues.

For centuries, remedies derived from plants, the wonderful gifts of our planet, along with ancient, subtle energy healing practices, were used with great success, without the need for pharmaceuticals. However, these practices have been reduced to unscientific magic and replaced by prescription drugs, which have rapidly become the preferred choice of the day because of their higher revenue potentials.

Interestingly, there was a time when a doctor practising ancient Chinese medicine was paid as long as the people were healthy. When there was illness, payment was withheld, as his job was to maintain health. Today's medical professionals thrive on our illnesses. The practice of paying a medical professional a retainer for maintaining health could be an interesting shift during the Age of Aquarius. It certainly would be an expression of higher consciousness medicine.

Today, there are scientists and researchers engaged in bold new studies linking spirituality and science. While Aquarius may not be the most appropriate climate for religion, spirituality or metaphysics, it is the best climate for science. Interestingly, combined with the innate curiosity of the time, science is reaching beyond the usual physical, tangible dimensions to the realms of consciousness, frequency, energy, mind, thought and vibration. What we are witnessing is the higher level Aquarian open-minded interplay of science and spirituality.

This does not mean that all scientists will embrace spirituality or that the spiritually-minded will decide to take up the study of science. Some scientists will continue to adhere to traditional religious and cultural beliefs while not embracing spirituality and some scientists will be neither religious nor spiritual. Each person will choose based on their comfort level and personal need for growth because—and this is a key point—each person's journey is unique.

We need teachings, knowledge and experience that will promote the expansion of consciousness for the entire human collective. We need to break with the past once and for all in order to avoid repeating the downward cycle. How many times must we go down the ladder before realizing that we are going in the wrong direction? The quality of life for all in the next era will depend on our mutual agreements on how and what we decide to do. Have we not felt sufficient pressure in the last couple of decades to warrant a claim for something different? Decisions and choices need to be questioned, and corrections need to be made. Hence again, the urgent, long-awaited and long overdue need for a major shift in consciousness. In true Aquarian style, we need to break free and dare to explore beyond the long-held familiar confines of the human experience and wonder if there might be a better way.

The One True Teaching

While researching new spiritual works during the pandemic, I came to understand a few interesting things about teachings, but one lesson stands out above all others. As a long-time traveller on the spiritual path, I have made pit stops at many schools of thought. At each pit stop, I believed that I had found "the one" or, more precisely, the one and only—the absolute truth. This pattern of devotion and loyalty to "the one and only one teaching" had clearly been established during childhood, no doubt a carryover from previous lifetimes. At Sunday Mass, the same prayer was recited, over and over and over: I believe in the Holy Catholic Church, the one and only church. Whether in English or in French, it was the same song: one and only; seule et unique; one and only; seule et unique.

In my teens, when I first began reading spiritual texts—mostly the lives of the saints—as a well-trained and obedient Catholic, I would check for the "nihil obstat" in the credits before buying a book. I certainly did not want to expose myself to unholy,

CHAPTER 3 · BREAKING THE CYCLE

unblessed, "unauthorized" works. When I eventually gathered up enough courage and dared to venture out and read books that did not have the Roman Catholic Church's stamp of approval, it was with a certain sense of security. I must be safe since I had been baptized and I belonged to the "one and only" church. Maybe it's okay to read Lobsang Rampa and Paul Brunton and Krishnamurti without danger of being sentenced to purgatory, or worse, hell. I am, after all, still a Catholic.

During the pandemic, I came across teachings other than *A Course in Miracles*—my latest "one and only"—that resonated surprisingly well with me. In fact, they actually provided the support and clarity I needed at that time. Then I hit a wall. While I felt very much drawn to some of these new works, I found myself reluctant to explore them because of a false sense of loyalty to the teachings I had adhered to and written about over the past several years. Uncovering and releasing this deeply entrenched guilt-driven belief in the "one and only" became an excellent healing opportunity. I suspect that some of this inner conflict may have contributed to the pain I experienced in my arms during that year as I prepared to write about topics not addressed in the "one and only" teaching. It's amazing how much garbage that 12th house can hold. Maybe this book should have been subtitled *Time to Take Out the Trash!*

Note that this does not mean that sticking to one teaching at a time is wrong. Sometimes this is necessary to ensure a thorough study and perhaps avoid confusion. However, when a course of study or teaching takes on a mantle of exclusivity, it may be wise to take a step back. Exclusivity may be seen as a safety measure of sorts, implemented by the lower consciousness self of either the student or the teacher, and perhaps both, as a means of being in control. The idea of "one and only" is exclusive and divisive, and therefore can never come from an "enlightened" or higher perspective. To cling firmly to a teaching, exclusive of all others, may indicate that you have reached a boundary that you are not ready to cross.

Truth is all-inclusive, never exclusive, nor is it competitive, "my way is better than your way." There is no "one" teaching; most teachings contain elements of truth. The truth will be found in many ways—in as many ways as there are brothers and sisters who are in search of truth. Truth is true, and it will be found at the root of any valid teaching but also at the heart of the human experience. True spiritual insight does not need to be attained through an arduous process of study or self-discipline, nor is it only found in religious or spiritual teachings. It can, and will, be found in whatever manner, in whatever language and in whatever form best resonates with the seeker. While the truth may be found in a book, it can also be heard in the words of a song, appreciated in the beauty of a blossoming begonia, or experienced in a simple act of kindness between brothers and sisters. Truth simply waits to be recognized by the willing soul.

CHAPTER 4

Standing on the Threshold

Nothing you have ever learned can help you understand the present, or teach you how to undo the past. Your past IS what you have taught yourselves. LET IT ALL GO. (ACIM, Ch. 14, p. 342)

From Knowing to Not Knowing

Here we stand, near the top of the ladder, on the verge of taking the next step down yet another 26,000-year journey. Is this really where we want to go next, or do we want to break from the past and, once and for all, explore other, completely new possibilities? Given the recent influx of planetary activity in Capricorn—the sign associated with all things ancient and traditional—perhaps we are ready to release some of the old. In this time of transition, we have choices to make. We can continue as before, maybe fix things up a bit, or we can decide here and now that we've had enough of what doesn't work and we want something completely different, something new. This is truly an exciting time of transition for humanity.

What will it take to get beyond this threshold so we can step into a far better, more enlightened experience for humanity? If we are to avoid repeating mistakes of the past, we must be prepared to look at ourselves, at our lives, at our world, with fresh new eyes, through a completely different lens. Fortunately, new and different are attractive features for Aquarius, so this might help stimulate curiosity and interest and perhaps even a desire to explore bold, new possibilities. However, given where we have been and where we now stand, if we want to make a significant leap, we may need to abandon some of what we have learned, perhaps even much of what we think we know. And that's where we find our first minor—okay, major—glitch: letting go of what we know.

Aquarius takes great pride in knowing. The words "I know" bring tremendous joy and satisfaction to Aquarius and are a natural part of its vocabulary. We have become adept at labelling things, systems, programs, people and human behaviour. The more names, labels and classifications we seem to have (Pisces), the more we think we know (Aquarius). Let's face it; we are rather proud of what we know—or, more precisely, what we think we know. However, this knowledge—knowledge in which we take great pride—is limited by our current level of consciousness and may have little or nothing to do with the next leg of our journey, should we choose to move to a higher level of consciousness. If we choose to explore beyond this threshold into the new, we will essentially be entering a not-knowing place, which is not a comfortable place for Aquarius. It will take a fair dose of courage, humility and patience to move into the unknown without the support of old, familiar knowledge.

In this age of science, technology and unlimited access to information, not many people are comfortable saying, "I don't know." If anything, this admission is usually immediately followed by, "Just a minute, I'll look it up on the Internet" or, "Hold on; I'll Google it." Again, this indicates that we are confident that we have the knowledge and information we need at our current level of awareness. If we are to shift to a higher experience of consciousness, we will need to trust that there may be an aspect of our Being—a higher "Self"—that is capable of far greater accomplishments than the physical, thinking human that we—without question—believe ourselves to be. At least for the time being, we will need to trust in the existence of and be ready to reach out to this higher Self without the support of mainstream science, beliefs or teachings.

While putting our faith in the unknown will be a giant leap for many and impossible for some, it will be a welcome invitation for a few, those few who have been wondering if there might be more to life than the cycle of birth, aging and inevitable death.

CHAPTER 4 · STANDING ON THE THRESHOLD

Are we prepared to question every belief, every value that we hold? Are we willing to forget what we think we know, what we think things are and be like the child, grab a bucket of trust and engage in simple curiosity? Are we ready to seek out experiences that will provide a broader, greater knowing, experiences that will be far more enriching and rewarding than the tired, old, limiting familiar experiences? Ultimately we must arrive at a point where we are comfortable with not knowing, which, for some, may be a challenge in the "all-knowing" Age of Aquarius.

Changing Times, Changing Needs

Teachings are continually evolving and changing to meet the needs of the times and our readiness for change. While many of the teachings in ancient as well as more recent traditional works may have been relevant for those times, this may no longer be true. In some cases, they may even limit or prevent us from rising to a higher level of consciousness. So it is that during this transition from Pisces to Aquarius, a call for a better understanding of life and the human condition has been made, which is understandable since the desire "to know" is an inherent trait of Aquarius. However, this call has a price tag: long-standing belief-based and blindly followed teachings may need to be re-evaluated, adjusted or even abandoned if they are to contribute to the current shift in consciousness.

While traditional teachings are being brought up to date, researchers are bringing to light certain aspects of ancient wisdom teachings that have been hidden, lost or forgotten over time. What is interesting about these discoveries is that some of the teachings being uncovered are quite relevant today and can serve to facilitate our present and future growth. This implies that we may now be ready to appreciate wisdom teachings that we were not ready to embrace or even understand thousands of years ago. We can only wonder how and why we lost these teachings in the first place.

Fortunately, we do not need to wait for traditional teachings to be completely cleaned up and updated or for science to catch up before we can engage in our own shift in consciousness. As we move into the Age of Aquarius, bold new perspectives are being shared with us, providing a broader understanding of our place in an ever-expanding life experience. With the advent of information technologies, any seeker can find the teaching they need to support their journey, no matter where they are in the world and no matter their current level of conscious awareness.

Spiritual or wisdom teachings reach us in two primary ways. The first is through channelled works. As most are aware, channelling has been used for millennia to impart wisdom to beings in the human condition, as found, for example, in the Bible and other "sacred texts." At the dawn of the information age, there has been a significant influx of new channelled works. The very idea of receiving messages from "beyond" is very much in tune with Aquarius, the Era of exploring where no man/woman has gone before. The profusion of sci-fi and space exploration (Aquarius) dramas (Pisces) over the past few decades is a testament to this fact.

Channelled messages are usually conveyed using language and symbolism that are appropriate for the culture and particular level of consciousness as well as the unique needs of the group receiving the messages. One important factor to consider is that channelled messages are received by individuals who are, for the most part, still bound by the human condition. The messages thus received may in part be coloured or even limited by their personal filters. Some of these messages may be very accurate, while others will immediately be recognized as clouded by misunderstanding, tainted by personal bias or merely fictional. The fact is that we all perceive through filters until we are fully awake. We must learn to recognize and then look beyond the filters to see the truth.

It is not uncommon to put channellers, teachers or "masters" on a pedestal. This is a deeply ingrained practice found in most cultures, and it serves primarily those in positions of power and authority. Whenever the idea of specialness arises in a relationship, it becomes exclusive, and anything exclusive is not whole—or holy—and cannot fully express truth. To see someone as a special holy person, somehow higher than or above you, implies separation,

CHAPTER 4 • STANDING ON THE THRESHOLD

division or distance between you and that person. In so doing, you deny yourself the experience of your own wholeness, or holiness. A true teacher will never claim superiority over another. An example is someone like Jesus/Jeshua, who will rarely be perceived as a brother or an equal, although he never portrayed himself as anything but an equal. He makes this very clear in *A Course in Miracles* where he says: "Equals cannot be in awe of one another because awe implies inequality.... There is nothing about me that YOU cannot attain" (ACIM, Ch. 1, p. 13).

Once a teacher or anyone else, for that matter, has become an idol, a sense of littleness and unworthiness has been established. This unworthiness, a common trait among spiritual seekers, is a clever fear-based ego or small-self device designed to slow down or altogether prevent growth. It may also serve to bolster the ego and pocketbook of the teacher. Beware of teachers who indulge in this kind of specialness, especially those who endorse complex, multi-level techniques, rituals, teachings and practices. A true teacher will always acknowledge, support and reinforce your worth and will always see the truth of who you are—an equal brother or sister, an expression of the One Creator Source.

The second way in which teachings are imparted is directly through the centre of our Being, through our own inner channel to truth—the higher Self. This point was made very clear when I recognized material from the notes I had been gathering in my journal in the teachings I was exploring. On a number of occasions, I heard channellers express the very same ideas I had already written, sometimes verbatim. I then realized that I had been receiving information directly, without the aid of a channeller or teaching. For someone accustomed to seeking advice, counsel and teachings outside herself, someone accustomed to handing authority to a higher, more knowledgeable "special" person or "master," this was a significant revelation.

Truth is available to every one of us—each and every one of us—at the very centre of our Being. However, we must first seek it and then be open to receive it before it can flow through us. More than ever, we need to lean into and learn to trust our own portal to inner knowing.

New Teachings for a New Age

Among the many teachings being offered to us at this time of transition is *A Course in Miracles*. Given its unique style and language and its radical, new perspective, the Course is an important bridge between the Ages of Pisces and Aquarius. The Course came into existence over a period of several years in the late sixties and early seventies, as the Pisces Era was waning and the Aquarius Era was emerging. It was given to us thanks to the bravery and dedication of psychologists Helen Schucman, who "received" the content, and Bill Thetford, who assisted her with the transcription. Bravery is an appropriate description for their work, as it records conversations held with Jesus, a fact that may cause some to question its authenticity or even reject it altogether.

Admittedly a voluminous work, written in a style resembling more a Shakespearean religious treatise for the academically minded than a contemporary New Age book on breaking through the boundaries to awakening, *A Course in Miracles* is definitely not an easy read. For many, the problem with the big blue book is its complicated writing style and use of traditional Biblical language such as God, Father, Son, Holy Spirit, saviour, sin, guilt. As one quickly learns, while the Course may use biblical or Pisces terminology, its message is anything but biblical. In fact, its message is radically different from that of our traditional teachings, as it reveals much-needed previously hidden truths and brings corrections to traditional teachings. At its core, the Course is very much in harmony with the transition into the Era of Aquarius.

As shared in *Making Peace with God*, I found the Course to be a very difficult read, at least at first, pointing out that it might as well have been written in Icelandic kilometre since the iambic pentameter was entirely lost on me. After having read through the entire book, I suspected that I had become dyslexic. There are sentences and paragraphs that I still find difficult to comprehend, but there

CHAPTER 4 · STANDING ON THE THRESHOLD

are those that resonate deeply with the truth that is emerging from deep within my soul.

It is helpful to keep in mind that each person's style of learning is unique. Throughout high school, I loved math because it was straightforward and simple, okay, maybe not always easy, especially those complex algebraic equations, but it was logical and fun, much like solving puzzles. An equation had a solution, and that was that; final grade: A. Words, on the other hand, had all sorts of meanings and interpretations, and it seemed that my interpretations of the literary works we were assigned were different from those expected by our teachers. Other than my paper on *1984*, I found it more difficult, actually nearly impossible, to get an excellent grade in literature if you didn't think like your teachers. Final grade: well, not A. Given my non-literary, mathematically structured brain, it was understandable that I would find the Course to be a challenging read. However, with time and persistence, it had a most profound impact on my journey.

There are many new teachings emerging today for those who don't feel drawn to *A Course in Miracles*, whether due to its complex sentence structure, intellectual approach or its Biblical language. If you are searching for answers, you are likely to encounter a suitable work for your learning and language style. As it is said, when the student is ready, the teacher will come. The book series *Jeshua, the Personal Christ*, channelled by Judith Coates, is very accessible and inspirational, as are the *Way of Mastery* books, also from Jeshua, channelled by Jon Marc Hammer. These may be an excellent alternative, or supplement, to *A Course in Miracles*.

The unique language and uplifting messages channelled by Paul Selig from a group called "The Guides" might appeal to those who prefer a less traditional style, although the messages are profoundly spiritual. For the adventurous, sci-fi-minded Aquarian soul ready to connect with beings from other dimensions, the works of Daniel Scranton in which he channels the Arcturian Council are inspiring, enlightening, positive but also very practical. Lee Carroll's channellings from Kryon is another noteworthy body of work. There is a heart-warming camaraderie and community spirit in his offerings, as he shares his platform with many channellers, teachers, lightworkers and even scientists, a perfect display of high-frequency Aquarius energy.

These are but a few examples of the inspiring and enlightening teachings that have emerged in the last couple of decades, and there are, without a doubt, many more to come. As our consciousness shifts, our need for information will shift, and again, more teachings will emerge in answer to this need. From what I have seen with friends and clients, each person will find the teachings that are appropriate for them, in their language and that meet them at their present boundaries. I've also learned that it's okay to explore more than one teaching at a time, mix-and-match information, depending on what you feel you need. The belief in "the one and only" has been officially trashed. What is important is that whatever you are learning is supporting your experience of a greater level of awareness.

Fortunately, the purpose of most teachings is to clear the way for a new way of seeing and for a new way of being. We don't necessarily need to understand every word we encounter. Their purpose is to dismantle outdated structures, especially structures of learning that are no longer needed or may even prevent growth and unfolding. Furthermore, to try to understand everything intellectually can actually be a delaying manoeuvre. As we move into the climate of Aquarius, we will find it more helpful to simply go with the feeling, thereby opening the door to knowing. As the Course says, seek only the experience, do not let theology delay you.

Choosing Your Curriculum

In the coming New Age, what lies ahead may not be the same as what is being left behind; what worked in the past may not be what is needed as we move forward. Today's new teachings are inviting us to abandon our old learning and try something different so we can more easily cross the threshold to a new experience of being. This is very much the case with these new teachings, which are designed to break up and release what we think we know so that

CHAPTER 4 · STANDING ON THE THRESHOLD

we can be free to move forward into new knowing. While freedom to discover the new holds great appeal for the Aquarian mindset, being told that we need to question everything we think we know and even be willing to throw it all out is likely to generate some resistance. On the other hand, one quickly comes to realize that this drastic approach provides the boost needed to get the shift of consciousness underway.

When first undertaking a spiritual journey, or what might also be called an exploration of higher consciousness, or greater awareness, there might be a tendency to gravitate toward teachings that validate our current level of awareness and beliefs, avoiding those that might push us too quickly beyond our current comfort level. This is entirely understandable. It is also beneficial to start from a stable, solid foundation before venturing out into the unknown. To facilitate growth, we must be sensitive to where we are so we can make changes and adjustments, as required. If we were to move too quickly, we might become discouraged and abandon the journey altogether. Being aware of our comfort level is a great learning opportunity, as it reveals our limits, our boundaries, which, once examined and recognized, can more easily be released. A good teaching may take you to the edge of your current boundary of knowing, but it will never push you beyond your comfort zone nor scare you out of your journey. It should strengthen and encourage you while igniting your curiosity about your next step.

There are times, however, when a comfort level may hold you back. You should not be so comfortable that you just want to park it and never move forward. When firmly entrenched and confident in what you think you know and inclined to automatically reject anything that is outside your current field of knowledge, chances are that you have parked it. Once parked, movement and growth have stopped. Ultimately, it is first-hand experience that is important, and this takes place when in motion, not while parked.

It may be wise to avoid taking on the challenge of a teaching that is too complex or too complicated, where it is clear that you will have to spend years perfecting it or working your way up through it. The goal of a teaching is not to become tied to it, memorize fancy words and master a practice. If you feel that way about a teaching, then it may not be the right one for you now. Even if it were absolutely true, if a teaching were to add to confusion, make you feel guilty, demeaned or unsupported, then it is probably not meant for you at this time, if at all. By the same token, this does not mean that a teaching that is difficult now must be learned and mastered at some future date. You may learn something today or tomorrow that will allow you to bypass the need for that teaching entirely.

Everyone perceives through their own lens, from within the perspective of their experience and current level of understanding, knowing and conscious awareness. The easiest way to come to a new level of understanding is through direct knowing. It is not even necessary to use words from a book. Use language and concepts that have meaning for you. By using words, concepts, images or metaphors that are a part of your everyday experience, you will be using words that speak to you, and the message of the teaching will be easier to grasp. Chances are that words quoted from a book, especially when repeated over and over again, will be less likely to support your emerging consciousness than your own everyday words. Even a sign on a passing billboard or a song on the radio may have more significance than a quote from a holy book.

While you may find arguments for or against a teaching that seem irrefutable because they are logical, this does not mean that the teaching is or is not appropriate for you. Logic is not the sole criterion for determining what meets the need at a given time in your life. In this period of rapid and radical change, what works for you today may not work for you tomorrow. Maybe today you need something that is not logical; maybe you need to simply feel something, let the tears flow, listen to a beautiful piece of music like the Mozart Requiem playing in the background as I write these words.

You don't study and learn the alphabet just so that you can recite your ABCs. You learn the alphabet, and then you apply this learning in order to experience communication through reading and writing. The same applies for a spiritual teaching. You

CHAPTER 4 · STANDING ON THE THRESHOLD

implement what you learn in your day-to-day life, and then you know. Ultimately it is not the teaching that matters; it is the learning and its application that matters. A teaching that cannot be applied in a practical way is essentially useless. It would be like reciting the alphabet without ever using it to read or write, or learning to count from 1 to 100 and not knowing how many bananas you put in your shopping cart. A teaching is only as good as its resulting outcome of learning.

When searching for a teaching that will meet you where you are at the moment, claim your sovereignty, since you—from your higher Self—are in charge of your journey. If you like, create rituals and prayers that resonate with you, in your language, using images that speak to you. Do what feels good in your heart. Enjoy the process as you uncover who and what you truly are. Remember, there is no one and only; there is only the one that is right for you now.

A worthy teaching will help you access true knowing in the best classroom of all—everyday life. When the new learning is applied in daily life activities, knowledge expands, thus leading to a fuller experience of conscious awareness for yourself as well as for everyone you encounter throughout the day. And since knowledge is not intellectual, it will feel good because love feels good, and love is an integral aspect of true knowing.

The best teaching is the one that may leave you stumped or seeing stars, but it won't make you confused or make you think and overthink and wonder and doubt. The best teaching may feel like it slapped you up the side of the head, but once the dust settles, it will feel right, and it will add clarity. It may insult the small self, but in the end, it will empower the true Self. The best teaching may include only one sentence or one phrase, and if that phrase provides a leap to greater awareness or takes you one step toward greater awakening, then it was the best teaching or book or source at the time.

Ultimately, we are the ones who determine what we will explore, learn and understand. We attract those teachings that validate and support us where we are now. If we desire to move forward, we will attract those teachings that will help us move forward. Whether it is a religious, philosophical, spiritual or scientific ideology of some kind, we are the ones who choose what is appropriate for us. No matter the chosen path, in the end, a teaching serves only as a vehicle to turn us in the direction of the knowing that lies in waiting in our soul, for when we are ready to accept it.

Since we are learning through our current filters, our learning needs will shift and change and grow over time. During this transition period, everyone is experiencing tremendous change, so our perception, our capacity to learn, understand, grow and explore greater conscious awareness is continually shifting. Clarity will emerge naturally as barriers are removed, and new knowing is allowed to find its place. As our desire for a better world for all of humanity is expressed, our filters will be dismantled and released until we can see the truth in all things. As our vision clears, our experience of the world will also change.

Sharing with Others

Several of my clients have shared that none of their friends understand their quest or their journey. It is not uncommon for veteran seekers to find it difficult to explain to others the message of their favourite spiritual teaching. Armed with the best of intentions, they eagerly tell close friends, siblings and parents about the incredibly exciting new teaching they recently discovered. They may even go out and purchase a copy of the Course or other favourite spiritual book for everyone at Christmas or their birthdays. To their great dismay, it isn't long before they realize that not everyone, if anyone at all, is curious about uncovering the meaning of miracles or is ready to listen to channelled messages from Jesus, Archangels or extraterrestrials. Not surprisingly, they are then accused of having joined a cult, or worse, they are labelled as suffering from some form of psychological or mental disorder. Trust me, I know; I've been there.

Being aware of the fact that teachings are very personal can help alleviate and even prevent the tension that can arise in personal

CHAPTER 4 · STANDING ON THE THRESHOLD

relationships when you discover a new teaching that your partner or friends or family members are not quite ready for. While a teaching may be appropriate for you, it may not be for others, at least not at this time. Once you begin to express your new learning through acts that reflect a shift in consciousness in the form of greater compassion and understanding, intelligence and relevance, those in your circle may become intrigued by what you have learned. This may ignite a spark of curiosity in them that may then inspire them to explore and reach out for greater knowing. But since this is not always the case, it is best not to expect others to follow in your footsteps. Instead, show them how it's done by example; radiate the love and shift in consciousness you are learning about.

Fortunately, in case you haven't figured it out yet, this journey is for you. I say "fortunately" because this makes it a whole lot easier, and it makes the road ahead much clearer. It's not that other people don't matter, since this journey is very much about our interactions with others. But the emphasis is on "our interactions" with others, how we see them, how we are with them. It is in the application of the learning in everyday circumstances, in the world, at the grocery store, in the elevator on the way to work or while driving our children to soccer practice that we teach. But, above all, this is also how we integrate the learning.

Still, now and then you may be approached by someone who is curious and wants to know more. For these encounters, you need to be able to communicate your wonderful new teaching in a simple, easy-to-understand, kind, loving and, most of all, relevant manner. As Jeshua shares in *The Way of the Heart*: a wise teacher first learns the language of the student. Otherwise, you may be drawn into an unfriendly debate when you suggest to one whose beliefs are based on pure science that you remember them from a past life in Lemuria, or suggest that they clear their karma so they can experience their adamantine particles of light. It would be pointless to recommend to an avowed atheist that they look for what God is being in that chair or in that smartphone or in that cup of coffee they are holding. If anything, you would be likely to piss them off and may even jar them into delaying their own journey, which is probably not the outcome you would be intending. Sometimes, it is simply a matter of changing up the words, which can be easily done when listening to that wise, inner voice. Knowing how to "be in a new way" with others is a key component of this journey since it is how we help all of humanity cross the threshold.

While working on the final chapter of this book, I pondered the isolation I had felt throughout much of my life as a spiritual seeker. This is not a journey I had shared with any of my family members, and I have had very few friends with whom to share the experience. One thing I have learned is when a question arises, the answer comes. It's almost as though the question and the answer are contained in the same breath. As I was listening to an audiobook, this little gem came in answer to my musing.

> In the awakening process, you usually encounter some resistance from outside of you. This may come from friends or family members.... Whoever it is that is resisting your awakening process, they are doing so because you asked them to before you incarnated. You wanted to have a voice of dissent in your circle because you need that in order to solidify what you are moving towards. Sometimes you need someone else to resist you so that you can dig in your heels and be absolutely certain that you are moving in the right direction for you. (*Ascension: The Shift to the Fifth Dimension*, Vol. 1, p. 37)

Which is exactly what I had done. Just a couple of weeks earlier, I had released all my doubts about writing on the subject of Astrology, changed the title of the book to include Aquarius, and forgave all those who had objected to my unusual career choice. I also expressed tremendous gratitude for all the help and support I have received on my journey and with my unusual career choice.

CHAPTER 4 · STANDING ON THE THRESHOLD

Tips for Studying and Learning

- A good path will be simple, peaceful, not overly complicated, and it will feel right.
- It will inspire you to be kind and loving toward yourself and others, rather than judgmental and fanatical.
- It will not push you to do things that conflict with your integrity, nor will it demean or belittle you in any way.
- Because a teacher speaks with great authority, it does not necessarily mean that they speak the truth.
- Following in another person's footsteps may not lead you in the direction that is appropriate for you. Use inner discernment.
- A good path will be inclusive. It is not selective; it is not hierarchical; it does not judge or condemn other paths.
- You will feel respected, comfortable, safe and supported at your current level of knowledge and understanding.
- It's never about the form of the teaching; it's always about the meaning it has for *you*.
- There are no right or wrong teachings; there is only what you need to learn at any given moment.
- If some part of a teaching does not sit well with you, don't feel obligated to accept it, no matter who the teacher is. Remember to let yourself be guided from within.
- Because a path is suitable for your partner, your family or your friends, it does not mean that it is the right path for you. Because a path is suitable for you, it does not automatically follow that it is the right path for others.
- If in doubt as to whether or not a path is right for you, leave it alone. If it is right, it will return, and when it feels right, you will know.
- A good teaching will sow the seeds of wonder and curiosity. It will inspire you to know more through direct experience.

Better than This

Painful memories
Lost worlds, lost loves
Future uncertain
What is the meaning of inevitable death?
No meaning whatsoever!
Where is the eternal?
Is there anything that lasts?
Or does it all just fade away and expire?
There's gotta be something better than this!
Where is the life?
Where is there hope?
For all of us!
Even those who don't believe in "spirituality."
Even me.
I despair sometimes.
Wonder when happiness will ever come again!
What is the ultimate?
Is love real?
Is there a source of joy?
I need something, I don't know what
But I do need something better than this!

Michael J. Miller

CHAPTER 5

More than This

[I]n the great heart of humanity there is a deep homesickness which never can be satisfied with anything less than a clear consciousness or understanding of God... There is nothing the human soul so longs for as to know God. (*Life and Teachings of the Masters of the Far East,* Vol. 1, p. 126)

An Alien View of Humanity

Imagine for a minute, maybe a couple of minutes—hey, why not turn it into a sci-fi movie?—imagine that you are overhearing a conversation coming from a group of aliens, highly enlightened beings from a galaxy far, far away. They have travelled to many places in this vast universe, but this is the first time they visit planet Earth. From the clearing in the woods where they landed, enveloped by a soft breeze, the sun shining warmly upon them, welcomed by the song of the birds chirping in the trees, they look around to gather a sense of how life has unfolded on this planet. Standing in awe, they all agree that this is truly one of the most beautiful planets of all the galaxies they have visited.

However, as our visitors begin to explore life on Earth, will their sense of awe be maintained? Will they be as impressed by our progress and evolution as we are?

As they begin their tour, the aliens first observe that the beings on this planet appear to be from one race—the human race. Like all expressions of Source, they are naturally connected and have the ability to share and communicate with one another. Together, they have the potential to express, manifest and experience wonderful things. Indeed, they appear to have tremendous knowledge, creative abilities, abundant resources and a wealth of ancient wisdom. They have so much to experience and so much to share! Clearly, this is a place where they must be thriving, learning and growing together as they care for each other and for the rich and bountiful planet that is their host. On such a beautiful planet, they conclude, humans should be doing rather well.

However, as our galactic visitors become more acquainted with life on Earth, they come to realize that, unfortunately, this is not what is being experienced by its inhabitants. Humans live in a world deeply divided by anything and everything that might wedge them apart: beliefs, culture, land, politics, wealth, education, age, religion, language, status, gender and race. In this climate of divisiveness, they struggle, compete, even kill each other to survive and maintain their little spot of separateness on this planet. Beneath this struggle is the greatest fear of all: that their cherished possessions can be taken away in an instant.

"None of this is necessary," one visitor says to the others with a sad shake of the head. "If they only knew."

Feeling nothing but love for their Earthly brothers and sisters, the aliens ponder how humans could turn this dismal situation around and make this a better world for all—the world it was meant to be—the world it can now be. It would appear that humans have forgotten that each and every one is a member of this family of living beings, that all are expressions of the One loving Source. They have forgotten that at the centre of every single being resides the most powerful force of all—love. Without this essential sense of belonging and without love, humans cannot grow and rise to their full potential, either as individuals or as a united humankind.

Our wise visitors know that since each being is free to choose their experience, and each contributes to the experience of the whole, humans will need to choose differently if they want to manifest something different on Earth. If they would only be still a while, learn to breathe deeply and release the resistance and the struggles, choose peace instead of fear, turn their attention inward

CHAPTER 5 · MORE THAN THIS

and reconnect with who and what they truly are, they would know how to turn the tide and rise to their greatest potential.

As our alien friends prepare to end their tour of planet Earth, they pause at the edge of a park where the townsfolk have gathered for an outdoor summer concert. Standing next to a sweetly scented flowering bush behind the last row of chairs, they listen in awe while the orchestra and choir perform Beethoven's "Ode to Joy." They all agree that humans are indeed capable of so much more—so, so much more.

"But," one of the aliens ponders while wiping away a tear, "are they ready to do whatever it takes to bring about this much-needed change?"

"Let us pray that they are ready and willing and courageous enough to do so," another replies. "We will always remain available to help in any way we can, should they reach out."

Who's Ready for More?

Many of the new teachings emerging today are addressing the call of the rapidly growing number of souls who are stirring, those seeking another way and who want to experience more of who and what they sense they are. Together we stand on the threshold between the old and the new, facing the possibility of releasing an outdated way of being that no longer suits us so we can uncover and explore a new way—a far, far better way—for ourselves, but more importantly, for all of humanity. However, while we contemplate making a giant leap into the unknown, each person must honour where they are on their journey since each person's journey is unique. Each one will need to choose for themselves when and how they will move forward.

Whether or not someone is ready for this step and how much change they can comfortably handle will depend in part on where they are along the path of their soul's journey. There are those who have enjoyed spending years, even a lifetime—and, for some, lifetimes—exploring various spiritual, metaphysical, philosophical and other teachings. These brothers and sisters are very likely to be quite ready and eager to take that forward step. But such is not the case for everyone. This is a point I sometimes bring up with clients, especially parents who are having difficulty connecting with their children or with those wanting to share with friends or family the bold new teachings they have found to be so fascinating and uplifting.

A normal lifespan can be broken down into three main stages: childhood, adulthood and seniorhood. From the perspective of astrology and numerology, it is possible to estimate the start and end of each stage. Since this method of timing is based on the birth date, these stages will start and end at slightly different ages from one person to the next. As a general rule, they can be roughly aligned with the 29- to 30-year cycles of Saturn and the progressed Moon in astrology, as well as the period cycles and start of the second and fourth pinnacles in numerology. In a general way, where a person is along their path is likely to have an impact on their availability and readiness to pursue new interests. Being sensitive to this fact can be helpful when trying to help a friend or loved one who appears to be struggling with challenging life situations.

The inexperienced, naïve, idealistic young souls in the first stage of life are most likely to be open to new ideas because their choices are still being fuelled by their natural inquisitiveness. While they are in the process of discovering their unique skills, talents and interests, their life has not yet been firmly mapped out. They have not quite "found their place" in the world and are therefore free to experiment and make changes and adjustments. Since their life is still in a process of unfolding, they may be open and willing to consider unusual, groundbreaking and progressive possibilities. "Yeah, show me," some may say, with a sparkle in their eyes. "I want to know more!"

Those in the middle stage of life are typically locked into the day-to-day obligations and responsibilities of grown-up life such as family, job and career. Contrary to the free-spirited inquisitive youth, they are less likely to be receptive to exchanging what they think they know for some radical new ideas. They have bills to pay and far more important things to deal with than spending time learning about some weird new metaphysical, philosophical or spiritual-quantum concepts. At least for a while, they may not be overly interested in the "big" questions such as, Why are we here? Who am I? What lies beyond the known? "Sounds interesting; I'll check it out when I have more time," they reply as they turn to more pressing matters. When, based on what we had discussed during the consultation, I suggested to a client that she might be interested in reading *The Healing of Humanity*, her immediate response was: "I'm not interested in healing humanity." At the time, her attention was focused on practical, personal concerns.

The third stage of life belongs to our seniors, or elders, who once held positions of respect in our communities. The town's elders were the ones we would turn to for advice and wisdom, a badge of honour that has sadly been waning in recent times. Imagine all that learning and wisdom acquired over the span of a lifetime now being overlooked and ignored. While many elders may be too tired and worn out to pursue new interests, some are wondering, what now? They have reached a point after a long and full life when the typical obligations of grown-up life no longer bog them down. Facing an imminent—and apparently inevitable—end of life, but still a little bit curious, some may be open to considering radical new possibilities. Is this all there is to life? What happens next? Could there be more? Standing on the precipice of this great unknown, some may be ready to risk letting go of long-held beliefs. "Why not," they might declare with a little seasoned boldness. "What have I got to lose?"

The Deep Yearning of the Soul

Over the past several years, I have heard clients express a deep desire for more, for something different from the age-old human experience, for something beyond the limitations of life in a body in a material world. While this desire for more has always quietly fuelled the human journey, it is now raising its voice and becoming difficult to ignore. Oftentimes, it is expressed as a vague sense of something missing, something not quite right, something just out of reach, something more that needs to be done. Interestingly, many of these individuals have never actively pursued a spiritual path of any kind. This means that the shift is occurring for everyone, regardless of whether or not a person has actively engaged in a spiritual journey.

As this yearning is being experienced by more and more souls today, this means that we—the long-time seekers of truth—no longer travel alone. The fact that we are not alone makes the journey all the more enjoyable. It also ignites our desire to make whatever contribution we can make—whether small or great—for the good of all. Together we engage in this great shift for all humanity, and in this togetherness, we are in alignment with the frequency of Aquarius.

Not knowing any better—at least not until this time of shift—most people have attempted to fill that desire for more, that need to fill the emptiness, with the acquisition of money, power, status, recognition, fame and material goods—all lower expressions of consciousness. Consider this: imagine that you have all the wealth, all the gold, all the money in the world—everything you could possibly desire. You have it all. But here's the kicker: there is no one around to share it with—not a soul. There you stand, alone, just you and your prized possessions. What do you really have? Nothing. You have nothing of true value. The idea of attaining fulfillment through wealth or material abundance is illusory, as it is based on definitions, valuations and agreements made between individuals trapped in a very low level of consciousness. It says that things, possessions, are more valuable than people, than life, than love. Satisfaction on the material level alone can never lead to true fulfillment.

Now imagine a world in which everyone has equal wealth and abundance, no matter their job, profession, status, education, race, gender or any other factor commonly used to determine worth. Imagine a world without lack, without the need to compete, beg, borrow or steal, a world in which each person is held in equal value and respect, simply because it is their birthright. Do you think that in such a world we would be talking about our wealth or possessions? Would we be concerned with who's got the nicest car or house or designer shoes? No. These things simply would not matter. What would matter is that we have each other. What would matter is how we could help each other by supporting, nurturing and encouraging each other's growth and unique expression. What would matter is how to live on this beautiful planet in a peaceful, harmonious, productive, creative and respectful way. In this new way of being in the world, the void, the urge for more would simply fade away. This is the higher level of consciousness that humanity is now calling for.

Although I have spent a considerable part of my life journey studying various spiritual teachings, the goal was never to become an expert on the subject. It's not that I like studying. I'm not an overly intellectual or studious person; in fact, I don't like to study just for the sake of studying. Yet, I have always been curious about the nature of life and especially what lies beyond what we know and experience as beings, born to live and eventually die on this planet—like tiny, insignificant specks of dust in an endless universe. Now in the "elder" stage of life, this urge to uncover what lies beyond the known has taken on even greater importance; in fact, my curiosity has blossomed such that it has become the fuel that guides my everyday life.

I often see this curiosity in the eyes of many of the new generation of youth as they express their desire to experience so much more than what they have been taught and encouraged to pursue. Contrary to previous generations, more and more young people are choosing to follow their hearts rather than yield to the demands of traditional and customary rules. For these souls, the need or requirement to please others or look good in the eyes of the world holds little or no appeal.

Some are beginning to have a vague sense that the world as we see it does not reflect what we are truly capable of, what we really deserve as expressions of an infinite, intelligent, creative, loving Life Source. In working with young people over the last few years, I have noticed that many are having difficulty finding their place in this world, in a physical body, in a competitive, materialistic environment, which, to them, doesn't seem to make sense. In a way, they are correct in saying that the world as they see it does not make sense, since they were born at a time when a greater sense of Self is beginning to emerge for all of humanity.

Born halfway through the last century, I felt lost, unable to relate to those of my generation. None of my classmates were listening to Stan Getz and Saint-Saens or reading books on saints and swamis. Having survived the "dark night of the soul" years of my youth, I then found myself out of sync with the New Age movement since, by then, I'd already been there and done that. As someone who had never quite fit in, it was easy to feel for the young souls of today and to just love them. When I mentioned this to a young client, she looked at me, wide-eyed, and said, "Wow, you must be the only one!" I chuckled when it occurred to me that I must have been the original millennial; only I was born a half-century earlier.

Why is it that so many souls, young and old, are crying out for more, even when they have no significant material lack? It must be that there is something stirring deep within our souls, a part of us that knows more than what we think we know. It is this inner calling that needs to be uncovered and given expression. Humanity has now attained a level of conscious awareness that will allow us to take the next step in our unfolding. No matter the age, everyone can reach beyond the current boundaries of the human condition and, should they so desire, experience more.

The Transition into Aquarius

As history indicates, the world does not change from one day to the next as we leave one era and enter another, just as it does not suddenly change as we leave one millennium and enter another. The ideologies, philosophies and teachings that best reflect the nature of the Era are the ones most likely to thrive during that Era. Just like in winter, you will do better with a pair of skies than with a bathing suit.

Just as one Era does not suddenly end and another begins, the long-standing, entrenched values of one Era are not entirely displaced by those of its successor. It would appear rather that one Era adds to the former so that the Pisces principles would have been added to those of Aries, a task akin to blending oil and water. If this is the case, then the lessons and values of the previous Eras become essential in determining the foundation on which the current Era is being built. More particularly, we should examine how well we have integrated the energies of Aries and Pisces in order to gain insights as to how well we will integrate the energy or vibration of Aquarius.

Aquarius, which is ruled by the planet Uranus, typically supports individuality, originality, liberty and freedom. Its energy is progressive, scientific, inventive and independent. It is a force that seeks to differentiate itself from the masses. Those who were born in the forties and fifties lived through the strong Aquarian influence of the major conjunction in Aquarius in February 1962. This conjunction may have sparked the initial drive for independence, autonomy and especially individualism that has now become part of the common experience for many people.

The recent transits of several of the outer planets in Aquarius, Saturn (1991–1993), Uranus (1995–2003), Neptune (1998–2011) and Jupiter (1997–1998) have certainly reinforced the Aquarian energy on the planet. Today, bookstores abound with self-help and self-awareness books all geared toward helping the individual find his/her unique purpose in life, a strong indicator of the emergence of the Aquarian climate.

The extremist militant/terrorists with whom we are becoming acquainted today are also the children of parents born in the forties and fifties and have no doubt inherited the same desire for freedom of expression and autonomy. Many come from backgrounds that have known war and poverty for many years. Aquarius energy can also be eccentric, radical, unpredictable, rebellious and impersonal. As a fixed sign, it can be stubborn, rigid and intolerant. Uranus manifests in ways that are ingenious, unique, unusual and revolutionary, but also can be radical, eccentric, explosive, extreme, fanatical and violent. Acts of violence and terrorism reflect the dark, low consciousness Aquarius and Aries combined energies.

An interesting illustration of the merging of Pisces and Aquarius energies is our fascination for stories about extraterrestrial foes, such as are found in *Star Trek* and other series. Here we have a clear example of the dualistic forces at work where our essential responsibility for what happens to us is displaced and projected onto an external evil (Pisces) using a hi-tech scenario (Aquarius). The cast of heroes is often multicultural (Pisces), and they generally fight (Aries) for freedom and autonomy (Aquarius). Perhaps our fascination with these stories is born of an unconscious desire to find unity, for in facing a common enemy—albeit a lower consciousness viewpoint—humanity would naturally be forced to unite.

However, what if there were a better way of bringing us together? What if there were a way that would allow us to express from a higher level of consciousness, one that was not founded on conflict, competition, war, selfishness or violence?

The Key to the Doorway

Those familiar with my earlier books are aware that this quest was ignited long ago by a desire to uncover the truth of who and what we are, to know the true meaning of life. There was always a sense that what was taught in school and in church somehow didn't add up. While digging through old journals for something to read at a writers' group meeting, I found the following entry. It was all the more remarkable because it was written in 1986, long before the

CHAPTER 5 · MORE THAN THIS

bold new teachings of today were available. It expressed a cry for a completely different way of being, a cry made by many young souls today. Here it is, as it was written, so, raw and unedited.

> It's a different kind of freedom I am looking for—a freedom from darkness, from non-consciousness. It's like never-going-to-sleep-againness. I want the consciousness that goes beyond the physical body. The one that can leave it and not be bound by time or space. I want to perceive with my "other eyes" my "knowing" self. The one that knows where reality begins and remembers it all the time. The one that does not become drowned out by emotions and conditionings and rationalizational mental processes. The conscious self that doesn't disappear in sleep at night between midnight and 8 AM, the one that knows what's right for me and doesn't have to ask what someone else would do. What does a Gurdjieff or someone else say?
>
> I want to have no barriers of time or space. The more it goes, the more I am convinced that there is so much infinitely more to the human experience than what we live. It's like there is a big cover-up. It's all a big hoax—none of this is real!!! It's like millions of "humans" or "beings in humanoid form" wandering around a small patch of planet Earth for 60 years or so, behaving like Pinocchio's with strings, fears, genetics, conditionings, insecurities, etc.
>
> I often get the feeling that directly overhead in the sky—out in space—the curtain of our dimension (known, that is) gets pulled apart and someone is watching us, probably annoyed and frustrated at times at our tenacious stupidity and ignorance.

I smiled when I read that journal entry. Seen from the perspective of today's new teachings, that young seeker was right on the mark. It was that yearning for something that lies beyond the limitations of the human experience, a desire to connect with the "knowing" self—basically, a desire for freedom from ignorance—that had fuelled this quest for the truth. She had great courage. At that moment, I felt a surge of warm love for that young soul—the young me—who, despite the absence of any form of support for her far-out, progressive ideas, never gave up. And here was the key, that precious moment in which I felt love for myself—one of the greatest of all life lessons simply put into practice. It is this very lesson that we must all embrace if we are to move forward and discover the more of what we are.

As shared in *The Healing of Humanity*, it wasn't until the age of 58 that I first experienced love for myself. It happened as I was rereading a section in one of my books while working with the translator. All of a sudden, there was this deep, warm flash: I loved that author. Wow! That author was me! I just loved me! Then I realized that I had never, in my entire life, even for one minute, experienced love for myself. Oh, I had loved my daughters unconditionally—I would have done anything for them—but I had never, not even for a moment, truly loved myself, thus depriving them of a very important lesson. Imagine the ambivalence of the young soul who is loved by a parent who has never truly loved himself or herself. Like many, I had felt satisfaction and pride for some of my accomplishments, gratitude for the many gifts that life had offered me, but I had never felt love for *me*. What a lesson! This was indeed an important lesson; no, it was the single most important lesson of my life.

Curious to know if this was a common occurrence or if I was the only person on Earth who had never loved herself, I began to ask some of my clients if they had ever truly loved themselves. Most had no problem sharing how well they had fared despite the obstacles and challenges faced throughout their life. Some pointed out their accomplishments and worldly successes, expressing how happy and grateful and pleased they were. They felt content that they had done well.

Not really getting the response I was looking for, I would ask the question again. Do you remember how you felt the day your son or daughter was born? If they had no children, I asked about their puppy or kitten or horse—whatever they had loved in their life. To illustrate the point, I would fold my arms across my chest and hug myself. Again, I would ask: How did you feel when you held your baby girl or baby boy for the first time?

Then would come a smile, an aha, an expression of sweet tenderness, raised eyebrows or an almost breathless pause. Of course, it felt wonderful. Once they truly understood—and sensed—what I meant, I would follow up with the next big question. Have you ever felt that way about yourself? Oh, you mean, have I ever felt that for *me*? After another pause, perhaps a deep breath, sometimes teary-eyed, astonished by the sudden revelation, there might be a shrug, a slow shake of the head, and the admission to never having truly done so. Of all the people I asked, only one could honestly say that she had felt that kind of unconditional love for herself. To this day, I remain surprised at how rare these precious experiences of true self-love are.

While curiosity, a desire to experience something different, and the courage to explore the unknown are essential requirements for making a smooth transition from the Age of Pisces to the Age of Aquarius, the one indispensable ingredient that cannot be left out is love. Why is love required? Without love, we cannot make room for more of what we are since the Creator/Source of what we are is Love. Given its great importance, it is not surprising that a common theme among new teachings today is self-love. It is the only experience available to us that will provide the feeling of trust and safety that will allow us to release our current boundaries and explore the more of what we are—the true Self.

In the current human condition, love is one of the most misunderstood and misrepresented of all human experiences. In most traditional teachings, self-love has not been part of the core message, as it has been judged as pride or arrogance. Also, one had to be deserving of love, which made this kind of love conditional. Self-love should now be easier to implement since there is less of a drive for establishing worth through competitiveness and the need to please others in Aquarius, and more of an affinity for the feeling aspect of the experience. Love is felt, it is not earned. Many people will struggle, at least at first, with the idea of loving themselves. What may be even more challenging will be the practice of expressing that love for all, for no reason other than love is the very nature of Being. We must reach a point where we can feel that love for ourselves and each other without conditions.

When I love myself, I meet God/Creator/Source where He/She/It is being me because God/Creator/Source is Love.

If we are going to explore the possibility that we are far more than what we think we are, there is no way around the fact that we will first need to know self-love. For some, perhaps many, this will take a little practice. Why do we need to love ourselves before moving forward? Without love, we will demean, condemn and judge ourselves, effectively preventing ourselves from moving forward and reaching out for more. The belief that love must be earned runs deep. How can I ask for more when I'm such a worthless screw-up? I have such a long way to go. That sounds like pride or arrogance. Actually, quite the contrary, it is arrogant to pass such a judgment on yourself since you are an expression of a loving Creator/Source, and the Creator/Source does not create anything that is worthless. These judgments are fear-based; they are expressed in anticipation of the verdict and punishment that will be declared once we find ourselves standing in front of the great, almighty judge. They are completely unfounded and can simply be abandoned, right now, in an instant.

It is only through self-love that we will come to appreciate our worth, the worth that is needed if we are to allow ourselves to rise to a higher level of consciousness. We will need to love ourselves for our efforts and our courage as well as our stumbles, our failures and especially our greatest mistakes. It is through the learning that these very circumstances bring into our lives that we are able to discover who and what we truly are. In this light, every circumstance, every situation, every interaction, every decision can be seen as an opportunity for growth and should never be condemned as a failure.

CHAPTER 5 · MORE THAN THIS

We must come to love ourselves not for our accomplishments or our achievements, but just because, just because the Source of life—Father/Mother God/Source—is Love. As we come to know love for ourselves, it becomes easy, even natural, to know love for our brothers and sisters, no matter how undeserving they seem, simply because that is the natural thing to do, because it is our nature. Love is essentially the key to the doorway that leads to that greater experience of Being we so long for, and in this Age of Aquarius, it does not take long to realize that love feels so much better than anything else in the world.

Exercise: I Want to Know What Love Is

Take a moment to be quiet, maybe sitting in a comfortable chair or your favourite relaxation or meditation pose. Clear your mind of any clutter, any things you think you need to do. Right now, there is nothing more important than being quiet. Close your eyes, or look out at a beautiful tree, or lay a hand on your cat or dog. Be still. Breathe deeply. Invite the love to infill your whole Being, that very same love you felt for your child or your pet. If resistance comes to the surface, maybe you regret something you said or did earlier in the day, and you feel that you don't even deserve love, simply let it go. You can deal with it later if it is still there. Let it go.

Now, hug yourself, and let the love fill you. Feel the love. Love is felt; it is not thought. Breathe deeply, and hug yourself again. You may feel tears filling your eyes, but that's okay. Let them flow. Feel the love, now. Let it infuse every cell of your being. You are loved; we are loved, and there is nothing in the entire universe that can keep this love from being expressed. Breathe; hug yourself again, and feel the love. Do this simply because there is no greater way to be with yourself. Being able to feel this love for yourself will clear the way for the experience of your true Self. Being able to love yourself will open the door to feeling love for others. It will make your presence invaluable in the world, on Earth, in the universe. Feel the love and feel yourself rising freely into your higher Self.

*I love myself as God/Source loves me,
and so the experience is complete.*

Mother Love

I sometimes point out to clients that the most challenging part of being a parent is knowing when to stop being a parent. Once a parent, always a parent; it's not something you just turn off and walk away from. I don't know if this is a universal experience among all mothers, maybe even fathers, or just for women raised in the 50s and 60s, stay-at-home moms, or single moms. All I can say is there appears to be an involuntary reflex built into the mothering role that is triggered when a meeting with one of my children is imminent; note that my "children" are in their mid-30s, so this mode is deeply rooted!

A couple of days before a scheduled get-together, no matter how casual or trivial, I go into scavenger mode, scouring the pantry, the freezer and the fridge for anything I might bring. I search for something that will be helpful, maybe even appreciated—although appreciation seems secondary to the hunt for something to bring. It's as though all of a sudden, a great famine looms, and you want to make sure that your kid doesn't starve to death.

While scouring, I found a couple of cartons of organic chicken broth that my vegan body was avoiding; a freshly baked batch of banana oatmeal cookies; and, of course, a fresh batch of sauerkraut. The purpose of our meeting was for me to bring mail that had been delivered to our previous residence; it was a tax document, so it was relatively important. Also, it was to hug my baby girl; she had just returned from a month-long trip to South Africa, and I felt the need to wrap my arms around her. A few days before our lunch, our Facebook exchanges went something like this:

Me: PS I can bring a little pizza, spinach/cheese, for lunch on Monday if you like.

Caroline: Okay, I will make a salad.

Me: I'm bringing sauerkraut and banana cookies. Need anything else? PS, want to go to Adonis before lunch? Need anything there?

CHAPTER 5 · MORE THAN THIS

Caroline: Sure!

Me: Which would you prefer: a litre of organic chicken broth or a split pea soup made with the broth? I know, mothers are a real pain!!! You just can't shake it!!!

Caroline: Ha ha ha, both!

So there I was on the day of our lunch date, half an hour before my train, knapsack already half-full with the chicken broth, cookies and sauerkraut sitting by the door. I once more quickly scoured the pantry and freezer for anything else I might stuff into the bag. The last thing to go in was the frozen pizza, the split pea soup I had made the night before, and a small container of black bean stew and some biscuits for my vegan lunch.

While walking to the train, loaded down with what felt like 50 pounds of groceries, I began to ponder this mother love reflex. I thought of all the things I had brought to my daughters over the years, realizing just how deeply ingrained this reflex was. I'm sure some of the stuff I brought had landed in the garbage, but each time, they accepted my gifts with grace.

This is when I understood. No matter if it came in the form of split pea soup and sauerkraut, the gift was just a container, a vehicle for the love that was being given. The soup and sauerkraut that were received with grace and no doubt a sense of humour—followed by a big hug, of course—made the gift complete.

As parents, we can't help but love our children, and attempts to express this love sometimes come across as awkward. Our children show us that they love us right back by simply accepting our gifts, without even raising an eyebrow—or maybe just a twitch. We have the ability to give love and the ability to receive it, and when the love is returned, the gift is complete. In the end, that is all that truly matters.

CHAPTER 6

Beyond Beliefs

It is time for you all to recognize yourself as the pioneers that you are, taking life on planet Earth to new heights, taking yourselves beyond where you have ever been before. (*Ascension: The Shift to the Fifth Dimension*, Vol. 3, p. 232)

Consciousness Pioneers

Let's say that some of us want to know more and may even be ready to experience more of who and what we are. We understand that not everyone will be ready to make the leap at the same time, and we're kind of okay with that; we get it, mostly. In a way, we are pioneers—consciousness pioneers—and although we're not quite sure where this journey will take us, we're ready to take the chance that this is where we must go. After all, change is needed, right? So, if we're going to move forward with this shift in consciousness—with this awakening to the more of who and what we are—where do we begin? What do we need to do?

It can be helpful—perhaps even encouraging—to note that most teachings underline the fact that for a significant shift in consciousness to occur for humanity, it is not necessary for everyone to "wake up" or become "enlightened" or to "ascend" at the same time. Nor is it necessary for everyone to be even remotely interested in what lies beyond the current boundaries of the human condition. There is no need to be concerned about those who tell you: Hey, if life's good, why change things, especially when we don't really know what this so-called shift in consciousness or awakening business is all about. However, while it will take only a few to get the ball rolling for all, each person will ultimately need to make that choice for themselves. The function of the pioneer is to learn how to experience the shift so they can be an example and show the way for others.

Because of their active participation in this shift, consciousness pioneers or seekers are sometimes referred to as "lightworkers" or "way-showers" or "masters" or, as *A Course in Miracles* refers to them, "teachers of God." By applying what they are learning in everyday situations—which is the most effective way to access true knowing—whether this is consciously intended or not, they automatically teach another way of being. Imagine you are on an expedition with a group of friends, and you suddenly find yourselves lost in a dark cave. You have a flashlight in your pocket while no one else does, or at least that's what they believe. They just forgot that each one was given a flashlight at the start of the expedition. Would you wait for someone else to abandon their belief, or would you pull yours out of your pocket and share the light with everyone?

It's up to the pioneers to pull out their flashlights and be the light in the world. In so doing, a new message is taught, a new way is shown, on a level at which it can be recognized and understood, in ordinary, everyday situations. Each person can then freely choose whether or not this way is for them at this time. Some expedition members might decide to close their eyes because they want to continue to experience the darkness a bit longer, perhaps as a learning opportunity. "Hey, this is fun," they might say. "I can't see anything, but I can hear and smell and feel so much more." Whether or not they believe it, everyone carries the light within their soul. In time, each one comes to accept and claim and express that light for themselves and for all.

The world needs individuals who are willing and daring enough to embrace a greater, higher sense of self and be curious to see what that will mean in the world. For those who are eager to move forward, the first step is to recognize the need, and the desire, for a radical shift in their consciousness—or the desire for another way of being. This interest in a shift is often the result of a long-standing—sometimes lifetimes-long—quiet inner nudging that suggests

CHAPTER 6 · BEYOND BELIEFS

or hints that maybe, just maybe, there is more to life than what they seem to be experiencing. For others, it will be motivated by a desire for something other than the pain or discomfort, whether emotional or physical, they have been experiencing. They want to be free to experience joy, freedom and a better life.

If we are going to be in a position to consider an alternative way for humanity, one that is very different from what we know now, we must be ready to set aside what we think we know. Maybe we can simply admit that we don't know what is really "out" there. This is a challenging step in a time when information and knowledge abound, in particular, in the "I know" climate of Aquarius. It is easy to be comfortable and confident in what we know, whereas it is not always easy to face the unknown. Yet, the niggling question remains: Are we seeing the whole truth? Could there be more?

The teachings emerging today differ somewhat from many of the New Thought and New Age teachings of the nineteenth and twentieth centuries. While acknowledging the existence of a benevolent, loving, intelligent universal God/Source and the interconnectedness of thought, mind and consciousness, those teachings focused on the exercise of mind over matter. This knowledge served to bring about healing and attract abundance and a good life for the individual and their loved ones. Indeed, this was a step up from the long-standing beliefs in and acceptance of a life of struggle, overcoming challenges and the need to earn the good grace of an all-powerful, judging, selective and demanding God. While those teachings focused on changing beliefs and thought patterns from within the lower level of consciousness, the new teachings we are now receiving take it a step further. We are being invited to consider the possibility of fully raising our level of consciousness from the lower body/mind realm to the higher, more subtle levels of mind, energy, being, soul and spirit.

The purpose is not to seek "the more of what we are" or the experience of "the more that is there" just so we can manifest more material abundance, ease and comfort for ourselves. We are being shown that we are capable of having a new, vaster experience with a level of conscious awareness that goes far beyond the familiar body/mind experience, one that will bring about a full experience of what is good, whole, perfect and loving for all. By all appearances, there is much more to be experienced beyond the "good life." Just how much more? That is something we will discover as we dare to engage a little curiosity—okay, maybe a lot of curiosity. But, wait a minute, maybe I shouldn't be too curious. What if I don't like what I discover? Maybe I can be just a little bit curious.

Only for the Curious

The next step requires that we examine some of our core beliefs, in particular, what we think we know and understand about our origins, which inevitably raises questions about who and what we are. How did we get here, on Earth, in physical bodies? What are we doing here? What is the purpose of this human experience? My life is tougher than my brother's. It's one hardship after another. Why is that? My sister is so much more fortunate than I am. I can't meet my basic needs; how can I be expected to be the light for others? We're here, we exist in an increasingly complicated, noisy and complex world, and now we are being taught that there is more to be experienced—in fact, far more. Why on earth would I want more? Whatever it is, it had better be good!

It is interesting to note that those individuals who have faced difficulties and challenges throughout their lives are more likely to be open to pursuing another way than those experiencing an easy life. Although this is not a requirement, sometimes we need to feel some kind of discomfort before we can even begin to consider something different. Not everyone was born with this calling at the top of their to-do list, and so not everyone is taking on the mantle of lightworker. Those experiencing a comfortable, abundant life, free of serious challenges and obstacles, are less likely to embark on such a quest, especially if it means that it might upset their lovely apple cart. This does not mean that they cannot or will never do so; only, maybe not right now. Rest assured, however, that in time, they will do so, for everyone is destined to experience the fullness of Being.

CHAPTER 6 · BEYOND BELIEFS

Held up in the light of our growing desire for a greater experience of who and what we are, some of our ancient beliefs may now appear to be contrary to the new direction we wish to explore. Since our beliefs underlie most of what we think we know, we may not be willing to release them too quickly. Fortunately, our innate desire for more carries with it a natural, built-in attribute—curiosity. Curiosity will be particularly helpful on this journey as we realize that what we have become familiar with about the world throughout our lifetime—or many lifetimes—no longer serves a purpose and perhaps no longer holds any appeal.

While engaging in curiosity in the Era of Aquarius, it may help to add in some trust and faith, at least until direct experience brings us the proof we need. Aquarius, after all, does take pride in knowing. As this shift of consciousness is likely to take a little while, perhaps it would be well to add some patience to the mix. In time, our explorations into greater consciousness will find the backing of science. In the meantime, we can still move forward with a simple, open-minded outlook.

All great inventions begin with a simple question: What if? What if it were possible to have a telephone that was not attached to a base with wires? We'll send that to the R&D department and see if they can figure that out. Or, what if we could harness energy from the Earth's magnetic field to run our homes and cars and provide all of our energy needs? Let's send that down to the R&D department. What if we truly were highly conscious beings, capable of transmitting not only thoughts but also our bodies beyond the boundaries of time, space and matter, without the need for smartphones, cars and jets? Is there an R&D department for that? Hmmm—Oh, that's me! I'm the R&D department—the pioneer in search of an experience of higher consciousness.

It has been suggested that we should be open and curious like the child, be from that not-knowing place and wonder what lies ahead. Imagine if a child came into this world knowing that when she grew up, she would have to get a job she doesn't like, work forty hours a week and pay the bills while raising three children on her own. Do you think this child would be eager to grow up into adulthood?

The happy child knows that a loving parent watches over her and will take care of her needs. She is not fearful, nor does she worry whether things will work out or be perfect. The happy child feels safe, comfortable and free to simply be curious about life, about what surrounds her, about all the adventures she can engage in. Every minute of every day, she sees with new eyes because there are no memories to get in the way of uncovering what is right there in the moment. Curiosity exists in a mind free of fear, unhampered by beliefs, expectations or the need to please others, and it is fuelled by the promise of delightful discovery.

By engaging in curiosity, we momentarily suspend thinking and set aside meanings, memories, intentions and desires. In that moment of suspension, we allow what is really there—truth—to be revealed. Curiosity allows us to wonder that maybe, just maybe, there is something more that I am not seeing, thereby opening the possibility of accessing greater consciousness. With a bit of patience and a little faith and trust, all the needed proof is revealed through first-hand experience.

On this journey of awakening, it may be more effective to employ curiosity rather than intellectual questioning and analysis and effort. It may even be best not to try to understand at all. Curiosity opens the way without barriers or boundaries or expectations, while effort implies boundaries or barriers or something to be overcome. When there is a belief in something that needs to be overcome, you are making the "something to overcome" real, while it may not be real at all. Curiosity requires no effort and thrives in an open mind; it simply allows without effort. This is what it means to be as a child.

The challenge is that what we are being invited to explore out of curiosity, out of wanting to know more—the experience of full conscious awareness—is an unknown—or, at least, that seems to be the case. There are no guarantees that any of this is possible—or that it even exists. Other than those supposed awakened ones who are channelling new teachings to us here on Earth, we don't have many, if any, examples of people walking around showing us how it's done. As pioneers, we are pretty much on our own. It takes a fair amount of courage to pursue a path that no one else is pursuing, to trust that it is the right path and that it will lead us to an experience of the truth. Without the sense of the love of those who are there to support us—our teachers and guides—it may be next to impossible to pursue this path.

It's interesting how easily we will say "curiosity killed the cat" when facing the unknown. Why is that? Perhaps it is a red flag thrown up by the small self warning us against the dangers of exploring higher consciousness. Don't be curious; remain in lower consciousness. You don't know what's out there. Maybe you won't like it. Maybe there is nothing else out there, or maybe you will never see your loved ones again. Maybe you aren't good enough, and you will be turned away. We pack our lives with that with which we are familiar, with what we know. This leaves little or no room for what lies beyond what we think we know, for the unknown. As we explore what lies beyond, we may discover that the "known" can be a boundary, a barrier to experiencing something far greater. Thus it may be helpful to have gaps in our activities, moments when we can be more alert and open to things that we don't know, with curiosity.

Exercise: Easing into the Unknown

Do something different this week, whether it is ordering a different item on the lunch menu or taking an alternate route for your drive home—as long as it is something you have never done before. It doesn't have to be super adventurous like bungee jumping or rock climbing; it can be something very simple. Sleep with your head at the foot of the bed; eat your dinner on the opposite side of the dining table; park your car at the other end of the lot; wear shoes that don't exactly match your outfit; eat breakfast at dinnertime; go for a walk around the block without your smartphone. Find fun ways to break up your daily routine.

While engaging in this new activity, don't think about it, don't try to understand or name or evaluate it. Get a sense of its meaning by simply being present with it; listen to it, feel it, and of course, open your heart and know it with love. It's amazing how much of what we do is programmed and habitual, all of which interferes with natural curiosity. Breaking up rigid patterns by engaging in activities outside of daily habits can prepare the way for exploring radical new ideas and teachings. It can be helpful to have gaps in our schedules, times when we can be more alert and open to the unknown, with curiosity. The more open we are to change, the easier it is to welcome and engage in the shift in consciousness.

In the Beginning...

What was in the beginning? Oh right, it was the Word, and the Word was God. Right. What the heck does that even mean? And this Word/God created heaven and Earth, including everyone on Earth, both good and evil. What kind of Creator does that? That's messed up! How can anyone in their right mind believe in this nonsense? Until science comes up with a better explanation, I think I'll just be an atheist; that's much simpler—at least, it's more logical, and it won't make me sound crazy.

Many people continue to hold an image of God as some kind of superhuman—make that super "man" who stands in a position of ultimate power and authority over everyone and everything in existence. They claim, teach and believe that we were banished from the kingdom of heaven for having disobeyed "Him." There are many versions of the story of our origins and many interpretations of this tale.

We have long been taught that there is nothing that lies beyond this life on Earth, that there is nothing more important than the struggle for survival and, hopefully, an acceptable level of success in the world. There is nothing after death except perhaps the disappearance of our spirit into some intangible realm, a great unknown, or maybe a vaguely comfortable, even joy-filled heaven of sorts. This pretty much sums up the core beliefs held by most, core beliefs we have accepted without question.

CHAPTER 6 · BEYOND BELIEFS

Very few of our traditional teachings express that we are more than what we think we are—just beings trapped in bodies in the human condition born to live and eventually die. Actually, none of the traditional teachings provide insights that go beyond this level of existence. The best we can hope for is some sort of good life after we die if we've been good, if we don't get condemned to hell or purgatory or some other form of infernal punishment along the way. For the most part, we don't give it much thought; who wants to! Our attention remains focused on our survival in a body in the human experience. And so it is that we remain at the same old level of conscious awareness.

If there is a deep-seated belief that what lies beyond the world as we know it is our "maker/God," and when we reach the other side and meet our maker we will be held accountable and punished for our errors, or our "sins," we are not likely to employ much curiosity about what lies beyond. Who hasn't committed any errors? Who wants to be held accountable for their blunders? That alone is enough to dampen any desire to head into the great unknown. These fear-based beliefs have been deeply embedded and strengthened over hundreds of lifetimes and may take a while to be released. The fact is that most of our traditional teachings, religions and thought systems were not designed to support awakening; they were designed to hold us within the confines of a regimented human collective. God did not make religions and teachings—man/woman did.

The traditional story of a God that put us here where we sinned—make that Eve sinned and the rest of us must suffer and pay for it so we can earn our place back in heaven—is not what we are now being taught. Thank goodness! If we think about it a bit—and Aquarius does like to think!—if God created evil along with the good, would not this creation have destroyed itself by now?

Then there are those who pray to God when faced with a situation they cannot resolve on their own. God has a plan, they say. He will fix my problem. Well, if God can fix their problem, wouldn't He fix everyone's problems at the same time, especially if he is supposed to be a loving God? If your children had problems, would you not want to help each one of them? In times of a world crisis, some will say, God has a plan for Earth. If He has a plan, what kind of planner is He? What we, as a human collective, are living does not exactly qualify as heavenly or divinely inspired. Is He just a poor planner? I'd hate to think of what He has planned for us next!

It is no wonder that as we shift into the Age of Aquarius, traditional churches are attracting fewer members. In this new climate, we need something logical and maybe, if possible, a little more intelligent and certainly less dramatic. We've had enough of the overcharged fear and drama that emerged and thrived in the Age of Pisces, haven't we?

Okay, Let's Try That Again. In the Beginning...

As shared in *The Healing of Humanity*, the subject I found most challenging to bring up was that of God. How do you talk about God in a "god-averse," science-minded, fact-based Era like Aquarius? While working on this chapter, I once again encountered delays; actually, several weeks passed before I could even begin to approach the subject. This time, the issue was not as much the wording as it was my understanding. As I explored the wonderful teachings that just magically seemed to appear in my life, I came to a more far-reaching and significant understanding of God, or the Creator, and by extension, who and what we are. This new understanding further strengthened my resolve to continue on this journey and, of course, get back to writing.

In a way, the less you know about God or the less of an idea or concept you have about God, the easier it will be to explore a radical new perspective on the subject. If you think you understand God and are confident in your idea of what God is, your view of another way may be tainted by that current understanding. Until we experience a higher level of consciousness, our understanding will be limited by the boundaries of current knowing, something we tend to cling to in order to maintain a familiar sense of control and safety. Ultimately, for significant change to occur, we will need to step into and embrace the unknown.

CHAPTER 6 · BEYOND BELIEFS

There have been many stories about our origins, but most of these should be taken as metaphors. As our consciousness shifts, the meaning of these metaphors will also shift. Learning flows with the movement of life. Many spiritual teachings or religions claim that there is an infinite, all-powerful divine God/Creator/Source and that He/She/It is the creator of all life, including humankind. Yet, nobody questions how humanity can be so far from being perfect, experiencing struggles, lack, pain, suffering and challenges of all kinds while the Source of Life is supposed to be all-knowing, loving, perfect and infinite. Does God, the Creator, make mistakes? There must be something missing in these teachings.

If we begin with the obvious, there is no denying that we exist; whether we exist at a high level or a low level of consciousness, we exist. We exist as living, sentient, breathing, autonomous, thinking, evolving, growing, industrious, creative beings. So, here we are, along with billions of other humans, plants and animals, on a planet we call Mother Earth, in an ever-expanding universe that includes countless other planets and systems, and, as scientists are now discovering, most likely, other life forms.

Before going any further with this line of thought, it may be a good idea to clear the slate of what we think God is. If we drop the idea of a thinking, judging, punishing, superhuman God, which is likely to occur in Aquarius, we may need to replace it with something more logical, something intelligent, a concept or an idea that embodies truth rather than the fantasies of our traditional teachings and beliefs. There must be a higher intelligence beyond what we, as the human collective, have been expressing on Earth for millennia. If not, we may be heading down a rather dark pathway, which is not something I want to face. You?

The Language of Truth

To facilitate this unusual journey of awakening, it may be helpful to examine our use of language. As we shift from Pisces to Aquarius, we move into a climate that will resonate with a language of its own. If we use words with familiar meanings that fall in the language of our traditional religions, teachings and cultures, words that are aligned with our current level of knowing and understanding, it may be difficult to conceptualize or even be open to a radically new perspective.

Words. This is a book, and a book is made up of words. Of necessity, words must be used. However, we all have various meanings for the words we use in our language. A seemingly ordinary word may trigger a happy response for one person, but it may just as easily trigger a sad or angry response for another. The experience of the word will depend on history, memory and the meaning attached to the word. Language is like a packaging of sorts, and it is easy to become caught up in the packaging of a teaching. Language serves only to convey meaning. It is not the packaging, the wording or the language that matters. What matters is the meaning behind the words and the experience to which it leads.

The use of words from language, religion and culture that hold familiar meanings may sometimes interfere with the shift of consciousness to a new perspective. It took more than ten years following the publication of *Making Peace with God* before I could feel comfortable with the word God, let alone pray to God. I found it difficult to reconcile certain core teachings from my Catholic (a notably Pisces religion) upbringing.

For example, I never understood the almighty God the Father portrayed by the Church, a remnant of the Aries Era. What kind of loving father would sacrifice his only son—and in such a horrific manner? Why did he have one special son? What were those terrible sins for which we needed to be forgiven? Since I've always had an inherent aversion to hierarchies that thrive on human inequality, ranging from royalty to slavery, I wondered what kind of loving God would grant entrance into the "*king*-dom" of heaven only to those souls who had been baptized and paid their dues to the "one and only church." When I was in grade school, I often wondered where all the "unbaptized" children of the world would go after they died.

CHAPTER 6 · BEYOND BELIEFS

Not everyone will be comfortable being called a "child" or "son or daughter" of God/Father, for not everyone had a happy childhood. While there was nothing wrong with my childhood on the outside, on the inside, things weren't as bright. Having engaged in a spiritual quest from a very young age, I never quite fit in. My feelings of solitude and isolation eventually brought me to that dark night of the soul period during which I would occasionally consider the ultimate release—death. However, while I was not inclined to commit suicide since I would be committing a "mortal sin," I was quite ready for someone to accidentally push me in front of the subway train or for a truck to run me over as I crossed the street. That would simply have been my fate. However, if there was one thing that kept me from committing suicide, especially after I learned about reincarnation, it was that I would have to return as a child. There was no way I was coming back in diapers! So, at least for a time, the wording "child of the Father" didn't work for me.

Those who have experienced issues with the language of traditional upbringings may find that replacing words that holds dark, heavy meanings with new words may make it easier to work with new spiritual teachings. For example, many contemporary teachings are using words such as Father/Mother, Creator, Life Principle, Abba or Source when referring to God. If the word "God" evokes the sense of a superpower—a sentient, thinking being, a wrathful, vengeful man ready to punish you for your tiniest mistakes—it may be a good idea—and it is perfectly okay—to use another word. This is your journey; claim the tools that work for you. Create new ones as needed.

Other words such as Heaven or Kingdom of Heaven may imply some great distance or a need to earn one's place just to make it through the pearly gates without being arrested and condemned for some silly sin. These terms can be replaced with Home, Reality or Unity, as they may feel more inviting.

If the language of a teaching is troublesome, try to capture the true meaning of the words. For a few years, I used the term Mind when joining with God since I had come to understand that it is through Mind that we are connected to the Source of Life. I also appreciated the Father/Mother alternative to Father commonly in use today. The God of my childhood gradually faded, and a new sense of God emerged—a loving, embracing, fair, gentle, caring, Creator Energy. The thought of God or a prayer to God should evoke warmth, safety and love, not fear, shame or guilt. It should be uplifting, inviting and hopeful.

You can test your language to see if it might interfere with an experience of greater awareness. Sit quietly in a comfortable chair. Close your eyes and take a couple of deep breaths. Bring up a word, for example, God or Father, and let the feeling in. Not everyone was taught that God was a loving Being. Not all women will be comfortable with the term Father. See if it brings up memories, discomfort, anger, resentment or lack of trust. Not everyone had a loving relationship with their father, and so to use Father as a term for God may not necessarily inspire a desire to get reacquainted.

The word you use to represent God should be free of fear or negative emotions of any kind. It should encourage closeness, trust, comfort, safety. If not, try another word such as Creator, Source, Source Energy, Supreme Being, Divine Source, Originator, Father/Mother, Allness, One Mind. If none of these work, make up your own word. Oneness has also been used in many ancient teachings, as it reflects the unity, wholeness and harmony of creation. You should experience a pull, a desire to join with this Creator/Source/God, for its essential nature is Love, and love, as we know, feels good.

When choosing language for yourself, be aware of veiled meanings. For example, when using the popular New Age term "universe," it can sound impersonal, non-sentient, absent of feelings such as love. The "universe" may come across as a cold, random or arbitrary force that is apart from you, a sort of unmanageable, even potentially dangerous, force of which you may be a victim. This kind of imagery could stir up fear and the need to be defensive or even take control. The word should feel warm, welcoming, inviting and wholesome.

CHAPTER 6 · BEYOND BELIEFS

Recall the love you felt for yourself in the exercise "I Want to Know What Love Is." If you can't feel it, do the exercise again. This feeling of love will be crucial to the shift toward greater awareness, as it will nurture the trust, the faith and the curiosity that is needed on this journey. It will also balance out the Aquarian tendency to seek out intellectual understanding before engaging in any form of exploration. The experience of the shift will be far more than intellectual. It will extend beyond all beliefs and, above all, it will be felt. If you cannot feel the Love of the Source/Creator/God, you are less likely to want to explore a shift that leads back to It.

In time, the words you use will no longer matter since language will have been replaced with knowing and, above all, feeling. Past experience, beliefs and memory will fade as consciousness rises to higher levels of vibration. You may then find that words that had once been troublesome will no longer bother you. Stripped of past meanings, they may then be used with great joy and abandon.

The language you use for your study and learning, however, may not be suitable in your interactions with others. You most likely will have daily encounters with friends, family members and colleagues who are not yet into this journey of awakening. It's one thing to engage in the practice of breathing in and breathing out God while you're out for a walk, a practice I very much enjoy. It's a whole other thing to tell your eighty-year-old Catholic neighbour that that's what you're doing while you're walking together. Perhaps you have made peace with the word God, but it may not be wise to tell your work colleague that God sent you that wonderful career opportunity; perhaps the word universe might be more suitable in this case, or maybe just say it was luck. Again, being intelligent in the moment is always what is appropriate.

I've Got the Power!

For thousands of years, many have accepted the belief that an all-powerful God created the universe, including the world in which we live. We have praised and thanked this God for His gifts and blessings, even for our suffering, our pains and our sorrows. We have begged for forgiveness for our sins, ready to take on whatever penalty we deserved, so long as it kept us from the worst outcome of all—to be damned to spend the remainder of eternity in hell. Believing that we have lost our innocence, fear of judgment and punishment, as well as feelings of shame and guilt for our mistakes, no matter how insignificant, became deeply ingrained. Thus was laid the foundation of almost every other belief we hold about ourselves, about life, about the world and the universe.

At the dawn of a new Era, we are beginning to wake up to the fact that this cannot be the whole story; it just can't! There must be more, much more. We can no longer sit back and blindly accept that a loving, intelligent Creator/Source would manifest a species of beings such as the human collective that would, millennium after millennium, continue to engage in selfish, loveless acts with disregard for themselves, each other and their beautiful home planet. This cannot be the species of beings that God created in His/Her image.

How is it that the individual particles of a begonia seed can come to life, unfold harmoniously and grow into a beautiful blossom without its various components engaging in competition and destroying each other in the process? How is it that a flock of pigeons—each one unique in its colours—can swoop up and down then turn on a dime, dancing in the sky in perfect unison without crashing into each other? How is it that nature can express such beauty and harmony while humans just can't get it right?

What if there has always been a Creator/God (insert your preferred word here) that has been creating all life beyond time and space, beyond all of our currently known dimensions, that existed even before the Big Bang? Then it might follow that what is contrary to Life, or Creation, may not be of the Creator; otherwise, the Creator would have self-destructed long ago. So we now have a new definition of God as a powerful, forever expanding, nurturing, creative and intelligent force with many attributes that we most likely cannot even begin to fathom in our current state of consciousness. This Creator/Source is the font of all Life expressed, including life

CHAPTER 6 · BEYOND BELIEFS

on Earth. If we exist—and our first-hand experience tells us that we do—it follows that we must also be expressions or products of this Creator force. We are a part of something far greater than we could ever imagine.

What we are now learning is that we weren't put here on Earth to satisfy the peculiar desires of a superhuman god who enjoys watching us struggle, squirm and suffer; we aren't here so we can evolve into beings worthy of God's good graces; nor are we here to pay for past transgressions—quite the contrary. We are far more than simple beings born in physical bodies that are destined to live as comfortably as possible until we face the inevitability of death. If you think about it for a moment, how could the infinitely powerful, intelligent, loving Creator/Source create anything defective, anything that is less than Itself.

We are learning that we are already whole, perfect and invulnerable, at least on some deeper or higher level of expression, that is, beyond our current beliefs about who and what we are. But more than that, as direct expressions of the Creator, created in Its image and likeness, we have been endowed with the very same divine or "godlike" creative abilities. At first, this radical claim requires that we temporarily suspend disbelief and perhaps just go with it. What if this were true? It would mean that we are not the tiny, insignificant, bumbling mortals that we believe ourselves to be. It would mean that we are the creators of our own reality—the world in which we appear to exist. I'm a creator—that's so cool! I've got the power! I'm a creator! Hard to believe, right?

But, wait a minute. This world doesn't look like anything an intelligent, loving, "God-inspired" creator would make; it's so not perfect. It's filled with struggle and inequality and all sorts of ungodlike stuff. This just doesn't make sense! So, what's the story here? What happened? That's a big question and a crucial one for which we will want an answer if we are to pursue this journey successfully. Having asked, we have been given answers, and for having taken that step, perhaps we should give ourselves a big hug.

CHAPTER 7

An Island Adventure

> In the Creation, God projected His Creative Ability from Himself to the Souls He created, and He also imbued them with the same loving will to create.... No Child of God can lose this ability because it is inherent in what he IS, but he CAN use it inappropriately. (ACIM, Ch. 2, p. 20)

The Power to Create

Okay, so, the news is out—God did not create the world, at least not the world as we know it. We, as the human collective, have been creating this reality all along. The bottom line is that our experience of the world is of our own making. For some, this will be received as good news; for others, not so much—actually, not at all. This can't be true; we don't have that much power. If we did, why did we create such a distorted, imperfect world? If we are so powerful, why didn't we create a world of equality, joy, peace and abundance for all? Is there any way to change this? I want to see a better world for myself, for humanity, really, I do. Is this something that can be done?

Those who are thriving and experiencing a "very good life" where all their needs appear to be met according to their desires may take a certain pride in hearing this news. How cool! I'm creating my own reality! They enjoy the world "they are creating" for themselves, at least until something goes wrong, such as a life-threatening health crisis or a stock market crash, at which point they will, without a moment's hesitation, turn and point a finger at someone or something outside themselves. While they may excel at taking advantage of the reality created by the human collective—of which they are an integral part—they don't understand that, as co-creators, they must also be creating the good, the bad and the ugly.

For the most part, not everyone will be thrilled to learn of their "divine" creative power, at least not at first—not without a really good explanation, and certainly not without a way of fixing it. The staunchest non-believer is likely to automatically reject the idea of taking responsibility for their creations, especially when things don't go as they would like. They will see themselves as victims of a genetic defect, polluted water, climate change, poor corporate management or bad government. Don't be ridiculous; I didn't create that for myself; how could I? Those with more colourful imaginations will blame aliens, dark forces, a hundred-year-old family curse, a gloomy prophecy or a secret society that controls the world. They have all the power, and there's nothing I can do about it!

The big issue is that along with this news comes the realization that we have played—and are continuing to play—a fundamental role in the creation of our lives and in the experience of our reality. Essentially, we are responsible for all aspects of our experience. Understandably, it is hard to believe—even harder to accept—that the imperfect world we see, as we are experiencing it from our current limited level of consciousness, is the world we have freely chosen to build, the world we continue to maintain. This means that if we are the creators of this world, we can't blame God, or the universe or any other kind of superpower or random force, for our world, our struggles and our challenges, or our less than perfect lives.

Those who believe they are victims of powers that are beyond their control are doing so out of convenience—the convenience of being free to point the finger away from themselves. The claim of victimhood is thus a way of avoiding assuming responsibility for one's actions, thoughts, beliefs and decisions. However, what is not realized is that while being apparently absolved of the heavy mantle of responsibility for their choices, they have effectively given away their power. Whether we like it or not, the fact remains, it's all on us. There is no scapegoat. So, how is this good news? It's so much easier to blame someone or something else than to assume responsibility, isn't it? But, I'm not sure I like where this is going. How could I create this kind of life for myself or for the planet? I think I'd rather have that scapegoat, please.

But are you sure you want that scapegoat? As beings created with the same creative power as our Source, we cannot be victims. By rejecting the invitation to accept responsibility for our choices, we also reject the tremendous power that lies at the heart of our Being, the very power that can bring about the changes we claim to want for ourselves and for our world. We don't want to go down that ladder anymore; we want to be free of it altogether.

As infinite creator beings, we have the power to create whatever life we want. A powerful creator does not see himself or herself as a victim. A powerful creator accepts responsibility for their actions, their choices and their decisions whether they appear to be successful or not. Through learning, the wise one will make adjustments so that the next creation will be better than the last.

A New Perspective on Our Origins

As we set aside some of our more distorted myths of creation, we are being presented with various stories of how we came here on Earth, as well as alternative frames of reference for creation and the origins of humanity. We are multidimensional or interdimensional beings; we landed here on a journey from another galaxy; we were seeded by space brothers and sisters. No matter the story, as our level of consciousness rises and our ability to take in broader, seemingly improbable perspectives expands, these narratives will also change. It may not be necessary to dwell on these stories too much, at least for now. If they feel supportive, encouraging and uplifting, they can be helpful, so by all means, ponder them. If they are frightening, confusing, demeaning and guilt-inducing, well, you know what to do: turn the page, switch channels or unsubscribe.

The knowledge of our origins will be remembered or come to our awareness, bit by bit, as our consciousness shifts and as we rise above our limited view and understanding of life on Earth as beings inhabiting physical bodies. It is not necessary to pursue a deep inquiry into our origins in order to experience this shift. Remembrance will come when it is appropriate, when we can handle it peacefully, without freaking out and running the other way, and especially when it is useful for our advancement. Furthermore, since we were created whole, from an intelligent Creator/Source, we do not need to learn how to "evolve" spiritually or in any other way. We simply need to accept the possibility that it is our birthright to experience our natural inheritance as whole beings, as mind, soul, spirit, light, loving and intelligent creators—expressions of an infinite Life Source. Then all that is needed is to allow it to unfold in our life experience.

Because the body appears to have a beginning, a middle and an end and we experience this over and over again, we have come to believe in a finite growth process with levels, hierarchies of learning and life experiences. It is then easy to believe that we must work our way toward enlightenment or somehow earn it or grow into it. We have simply forgotten that there is more to us than our current physical experience. Wholeness, perfection, eternal life can never be made less than whole, perfect and eternal, and so it is accessible now. However, while it does not need to be earned, it must be considered as a possibility, something that may take a little convincing or at least a fair amount of curiosity. For to know the truth of who and what we are, it must be lived.

One radical point on which there is consensus in present-day teachings is that we have come to the physical 3-D, body/mind Earth experience by choice. We have chosen to take form as a learning opportunity, to discover who and what we truly are as expressions of Source. Why have we chosen this? Simply because we have the freedom to do so, out of curiosity, just for the experience. With the use of our innate creative power, imagination, abundant curiosity and adventurous spirits, we have been creating our reality for thousands of lifetimes. From these experiences, we have learned much, and our learning is shared with other life forms in the universe. The important point about this revelation is that we always remain free to use our creative powers in any way we desire, whether appropriately or inappropriately, intelligently or unintelligently, lovingly or unlovingly. That's on us; we make that choice.

We have used our freedom to create, play, explore and experiment to our heart's content. Together, we have built a captivating world by making agreements: this is how it is; this is how it should be; this is allowed, that is not permitted. Our amazing industriousness, our ability to invent tools, technology and gadgets of all sorts, our creative expressions through the arts, the many ways we have devised to manage our various systems, from agricultural to socio-economic, are testaments to the creative power that lies within us. This indeed shows how powerful we are—a clear indication of how we are made in the Creator's image and likeness. So, why are we creating a "reality" that seems so imperfect, so fraught with struggle, pain, sorrow and never-ending challenges?

An Island of Separation

Since the dawn of our appearance on Mother Earth, we have enjoyed the thrill, the challenges, the adventure, the discovery, the learning and the excitement of life in the human condition, even when accompanied by pain, suffering or discomfort of any kind. Our long-standing courage and dedication for this brave journey deserves praise, not judgment, condemnation or criticism. Over time, we grew more and more engaged in this fascinating experiment of life on Earth. While our attention became increasingly focused on creating a good life for ourselves, on learning to deal with challenges and overcoming obstacles in the body/mind dimension, we forgot all about our "divine" Creator origins. We weren't banished from the kingdom of heaven, for, what kind of loving Mother/Father would banish Her/His children from Home? If that were even possible, we might as well give up now. Who wants to go back to that kind of Home!

We simply forgot that we made the choice for our human adventure long ago. It is in this forgetting that we began to alienate ourselves from our God/Source, from the Oneness that is the foundation and ongoing source of our existence. Captivated by our little adventure, we created for ourselves an imaginary tiny, fantasy island right in the middle of the infinite Ocean of Creation. It is as though we momentarily pressed "pause" on Reality so we could create our own version of reality and do things our way. As *A Course in Miracles* says, to think that it was possible to exist apart from Oneness was nothing more than a "tiny, mad idea." We set aside the memory of our origins as whole creator beings, as unique, integral aspects of Oneness, in favour of an experience of "twoness," or duality, a momentary experience of separation from Reality.

We are now experiencing the consequences of this timeout from Reality—what has been referred to as "the fall" and is now being referred to as "separation from Source." In the process of forgetting where we came from and what we are in truth as creator beings, we descended to lower levels of consciousness, further limiting ourselves to an increasingly densified and limited body/mind experience. The result is that we became divided within ourselves. We completely forgot about our true Self—our divine, or higher Self, or what is also called our Christ Self, Monad or Christ Consciousness. In time, we aligned with a less enlightened, lower consciousness version of ourselves, a body-identified, independent, three-dimensional, thinking self—the ego, or "small" self.

As integral parts of the movement of Creation, we have not for an instant lost the ability to create in harmony with that movement. However, when we function apart from Source or Oneness and align with the small, separated self, our ability to create is significantly diminished. The ego's domain is extremely small, as it is mainly focused on tending to its survival in the lower dimensions of the physical universe. The sensory, body/mind experience is so powerful that it is hard not to come to believe that we are bodies and that our life is contained within the lifespan of this physical body. However, it is powerful only because we have forgotten the extent of our potential experience as creator beings. For the most part, until we consciously make a different choice and reach up and claim our true Self, our Christ Self or higher Self, the world we appear to be experiencing will remain within the domain—and under the dominion—of the ego, or the small, separated self.

Living in Separation

The physical body is a highly significant component of the separation experiment, as it appears to create a tangible boundary that separates us from everything and everyone else, even from our Creator/Source. While nothing can exist outside of Reality/Creation, the 3-D body/form experience provides a temporary, illusory sense of separateness that validates the autonomy and independence upon which the small self is built and, above all, thrives. Essentially, the physical body validates the ego's separation adventure.

In time, we have become addicted to the sensory data generated by the body as it strengthens the physical boundaries and substantiates our existence in the lower dimensions, seemingly apart from Source. Even illness serves a purpose from the perspective of the small self, actually more so than the absence of illness since it further brings attention to the body. Sensory stimulation also serves as a convenient distraction from the inevitable discomfort of being cut off from the full experience of wholeness, peace and loving nurturance that always remains available to the "unseparated" true Self. But I have things to tend to right here on the physical level. I don't have time to look for something I can't see, touch or feel! Maybe later, when things are a little quieter.

But things are not getting quieter. As the tiny, inner voice of the true Self calls for our attention, the ego becomes anxious. Separation is not natural and therefore is not sustainable. The small self knows this and must work hard to maintain the sense of separateness on which its seeming existence is based. This is evidenced by the ongoing need to protect whatever we value, from beliefs to material things.

Separation is practised in many ways by the human collective. In our world, we divide ourselves into groups based on gender, family, culture, race, country, economic status, religious beliefs, etc. We create boundaries around our communities, towns and countries, and then work hard at maintaining them, making up clever reasons and justifications for their presence. Through our boundaries, we unwittingly push the "other" away, constantly reinforcing the concept of separation. Since separation is not natural in Reality, maintaining these illusory boundaries requires struggle and effort, even conflict and war.

We have effectively separated the Creator-expressed true Self from the imaginary, body-identified small self, or ego, both within ourselves and in our brothers and sisters. From this sense of duality, while we choose to see through the limited lens of the small self, we cannot truly know ourselves or our brothers and sisters as the divine ones we truly are. Since the small self does not represent who we are as expressions of the infinite Life Principle, it is understandable that we have developed survival strategies that are centred on the limited perspective of the ego. This has resulted in the lack of loving support, inclusion and respect for all life that is encountered here on Earth.

We have attributed great importance to dualistic concepts such as good and evil, dark and light, right and wrong, Heaven and Earth, life and death. Without darkness, we say, how can there be light? But, you may now ask, where there is light, can darkness take it away? We see things as black or white, one or the other, me or you, us versus them, our team versus your team, our product versus the competitor's product, this culture versus that culture, this religion versus that religion, my God versus your God, this country versus that country. Divisiveness runs deep in the culture and fabric of the human collective. We have even separated male and female, causing us to forget that Yin and Yang work together in perfectly balanced harmony. Without this balanced harmony, creation cannot flow properly.

The descent and subsequent densification into the limited 3-D level gave rise to the struggle for survival and the inevitable deeply ingrained fear that comes from being cut off from our Creator/Source. Once the belief in separation has been accepted and established as our primary operating system, we must then undertake for

CHAPTER 7 · AN ISLAND ADVENTURE

ourselves the meeting of all our needs. As has been shown throughout history, some will fare far better than others in the meeting of these needs.

In a world of duality, in the absence of a true sense of Unity, for the most part, everyone will be out for themselves, or at least for the ones belonging to their special chosen group. Some have been known to accumulate and hoard and even steal from others to meet these needs as well as satisfy their desire for more possessions. This low consciousness practice of valuing matter over spirit based on the fear of lack was strengthened during the Era of Taurus.

While we remain in alignment with the small self, we work hard at and delight in overcoming the challenges and obstacles encountered in the separated state for, here again, our existence is validated. The ego likes and needs to struggle, for that is its purpose as an unnatural, artificial intruder. Even in defeat, the small self has been validated, for it is then a victim of a force outside itself. The separated self is defined by its ability to claim, fight and maintain a place for itself in the world, independently from Source. The competition, fighting and even killing engaged in for the purpose of accumulating goods, money, land, power or whatever was perceived of value in the state of separation was amplified throughout the Era of Aries.

The separated self loves drama, as it implies potential threat and danger, further validating its supposed existence. It thrives on drama and actually defines itself by the intensity of the drama that it is experiencing. The absence of threat or need for defence will appear boring, unworthy of the ego—no drama, no life; great drama, great life. Whether the drama is positive or negative, it feeds and enlivens the low consciousness egoic state. The drama we see in the world is drama we are creating, sustaining and feeding because we, identifying as small self, love drama as it makes us feel alive. Drama was greatly intensified in the human experience throughout the Era of Pisces.

The Cost of Separation

As a result of our choice for an independent adventure into separation, we have lost our sense of connection with the Source of Life, a connection that provides ongoing access to infinite abundance, wholeness, perfect health, joy, love and a true sense of purpose and belonging. Note that we have only lost our "sense" of connection, our remembrance of the true Source of our existence; we have not actually lost the connection, for that connection can never be broken. In Reality, scarcity, lack, danger, threat do not exist; there is only wholeness, love, light and abundance.

The choice for and eventual acceptance of the belief in separation created a void that could only lead to an experience of lack. Life for the separated individual is then focused on the meeting of apparent needs. The world as we perceive it is thus based on principles of individual lack and need rather than infinite abundance for all. What has been forgotten is that infinity, by definition, cannot generate or sustain even a hint of lack. Even if some traditional religions praise the abundance of their version of God, this abundance usually must be earned, sometimes at the cost of the abundance of others. Once the belief in separation from Source has been accepted as truth, infinite abundance has been denied expression as a fundamental attribute of our life experience. We have effectively exchanged an experience of infinite abundance for a constant quest to address lack.

A consequence of this adventure in separation from Source is that we believe that we must now go after the meeting of our own needs. The ego, or small self, gladly steps up to the plate and gets busy with the meeting of what appear now as very real needs. In a mindset of separation, everyone is out for themselves. In addition to protecting its boundaries, the ego must continually work at meeting these needs, an activity that gives it a sense of power and authority, again, further validating its existence. The separated self says, I can meet my needs myself; I don't have to rely on the Infinite Life Principle or God or Source. I can do it myself, even if it causes me pain, or even if there is great struggle, or even if I must wrest it from others, I can do it. The ego thus stakes much of its existence on our belief in scarcity. As long as there are needs to be met, the ego has an important function in our lives. The more needs, the more challenges; the more the ego rises to the occasion and overcomes the challenges, the more satisfaction the ego derives from its independent, autonomous action.

Every Breath You Take

Desire is a natural expression of the movement of Life. It is an aspect of Being, and Being is always in motion, always unfolding and expanding. Curiosity is an expression of desire—the desire to experience something new. In fact, every breath we take is an expression of desire—the desire to experience Life. When we connect to Source Energy and allow Life to flow naturally, the needs that arise out of our desires to explore and expand our experience will naturally be met. If I want to know more, more will be known through direct experience. If I want to be more of who and what I am, opportunities will be encountered allowing the true Self to be expressed.

For some, desire is perceived as unwelcome, not spiritual, even sinful, and so they may work hard at repressing their desires. If you want to be worthy of God's love you must give up all desire, or so they have been taught. What they do not realize is that they are wilfully expressing a desire to not have any desires. Denial of a desire does not remove the desire; it only creates an experience of repression, a deepening of the sense of lack. This is usually done to reinforce self-deprecating beliefs. Oh no, you don't deserve this. Don't even try. The truth is that at its core, our life is the expression of a divine Desire. If we exist at all, it is because we, at the soul or higher level, had the desire for this Earthly experience.

Desires that arise out of fear of lack or scarcity are based on the belief in separation and are concocted and amplified by the ego. To turn to, or connect with, or even worse, depend upon, the Creator/Source for the fulfillment of our needs is insulting and frightening to the ego. Should you successfully have the experience of seeing your needs met by turning to God/Source, then the ego will have lost its important function as fulfiller of your desires. You will thus be undermining its power and position of authority in your life. What will it do then? Its very existence is founded on lack. However, the only lack is the lack of connection with Source, and that is only a momentary, imaginary lack.

A simple way to identify whether a desire is being expressed by the small self or by the true Self is to ask what the source of this desire is. If there is a feeling of peace, love, joy and perhaps even a sense of excitement in being of service to others, or at the possibility of making a new discovery, then clearly the desire came from the higher Self. If, on the other hand, there are strong emotions, fear of lack, a sense of having to do something so you can look good, or beat out the competition, a drive to fulfill a desire at all costs, this desire was expressed by the ego self. Once you have identified the source of the desire, you are then free to choose whether or not you will follow through with it.

You Have Everything You Need

To believe in or accept lack or limitations of any kind is to believe that there is a boundary between you and the infinite abundance of God, Creator/Source. I'm on my own; God doesn't even know me. He doesn't give me what I want; how can I trust Him, let alone love Him! The quickest way to remedy this condition is to simply abandon the belief that infinite abundance can be limited or made to be less than infinite. By definition, unlimited, infinite abundance cannot be constrained or withheld in any way, otherwise it would not be infinite. Abundance simply flows from the eternal Source. Are we curious enough to wonder if this is true? What if I were connected to Source? What if there were no more lack? Maybe this is something I want to explore.

We are now learning that, given our innate connection to Source, our true nature is abundant. When we try to fill the lack ourselves as separated egos, we are actually pushing away and limiting access

CHAPTER 7 · AN ISLAND ADVENTURE

to this infinite abundance. It's not a matter of focusing our thoughts with the intention of attracting abundance; it's a matter of taking our minds off the belief in scarcity. It is natural to experience abundance. In what is expressed by Creator/Source Energy, there cannot be any lack, scarcity, suffering, illness or want of any kind. There is only the experience of the fullness of Being. This fullness is not a half-full experience; it is Full. As we turn to the Source of our Being, the Source of Life, we will know that needs will simply be met. It is the intrinsic nature of Life to fulfill Itself; that is its purpose.

All that is needed is to turn our attention inward to where abundance resides. To turn to God/Source for the meeting of needs will no doubt be humiliating for the small self. But for the true Self, it is an experience of exuberant, joyful liberation. When allowed, Source Energy provides infinite, never-ending abundance, wholeness, perfect health, love and a true sense of purpose. In the infinite Mind, there are no actual needs, and there is no lack. Whatever is needed to unfold or move and express the infinite Mind appropriately is always present and available.

I received this bit of guidance when I had questions on how to meet my everyday needs. "Your needs will be attended to, and this frees you up to be open and available to help others. This allows you to be appropriately available for the growing interaction with the world and universe around you. This is the full practical implication of one of your favourite phrases, 'I am here to serve.' When you are here to serve, and you abandon the practice of wilfully directing your life or wilfully attributing a purpose to your life, then you are truly available to serve fully."

Needing a little break from writing, I was curious to know if adding peanut butter to my chocolate fudge cake would be good. To follow through with this experiment required the "need" for several ingredients. One bit of guidance I have very often received is: "You have everything you need." This is so true. Sometimes while making a grocery list, I have a hunch to dig through my pantry, and there I find the item just added to the list. As I had everything needed, including the peanut butter, I took some time out in the kitchen and created my new recipe. FYI, the cake turned out rather well, even getting two thumbs up from a friend who had cringed, shaking her head in horror at the very idea of the chocolate-peanut butter combination.

I was nudged by the inner voice to include these next two experiences, and despite my hesitation, I did as asked.

One day, while shopping at Costco with an elderly neighbour, we found ourselves standing in front of a table piled high with capri pants. We had spent a good five minutes going through the piles, pair after pair, looking for one in her desired size and colour. No luck. I was a little disappointed that we had not found what she needed. With my hand resting on the pile nearest me, I turned to her and asked: "What size did you want?" It was strange that I would ask her this question since I already knew the answer. Nonetheless, I asked. "Medium," she replied. I turned and lifted my hand, and to our great surprise and joy, there was a pair in her size and colour. Go figure.

On another occasion, I couldn't find the tracking slip for a package I had mailed to my daughter. I searched the small cabinet at the entrance where I put my hat and gloves, then went through my purse and my knapsack. Nothing. I did this several times, even turning the knapsack inside out. No luck. It must have fallen out of my knapsack when I was at the grocery store. I let it go, trusting that the package would arrive safely without the need for tracking. Then, on a hunch, I returned to the cabinet by the entrance and opened the door. There was the tracking sheet on top of everything else. I could not have missed it since it was on top of everything I had been searching through. Go figure.

Had we just missed that pair of pants on top of the pile the first time around? Who knows. Had that piece of paper been there all along? I doubt it, but there it was. In both cases, after letting go, needs had been met. I have everything I need. This is a very big lesson, one that I remind myself of every day.

CHAPTER 7 • AN ISLAND ADVENTURE

The Illusory Basis of Fear

The small self is very clever, as it should be since it is an aspect—albeit a tiny, misguided aspect—of great creator beings. Its unlimited cleverness is used to capture and maintain the attention of beings that are essentially infinite and have never lost their true Self, beings that could at any moment turn their attention to the true Self—beings otherwise known as Daughters and Sons of Mother/Father God or direct expressions of Creator/Source Energy. Because its existence is based on the belief that it is possible to function independently from Source and is thus not founded in Reality, it remains vulnerable to one threat: our realization that it is nothing but a tiny, incomplete sense of self. The ego is therefore always fearful for its existence because it is a false existence.

In our state of separation and alignment with the small self, we cannot help but feel a certain discomfort, as we are disconnected from our true Self, from our wholeness. In this state, we have accepted teachings that have led us to believe that we have actually done something wrong, that we have sinned, and that one day we will no doubt be found guilty and be made to suffer and pay for our transgressions. With these beliefs, a deep fear of God and what lies beyond the known has been instilled. It is not possible to exist apart from Source, so what we do on our tiny made-up island of separation has no impact on Reality. Other than in a few obscure, ancient teachings, until today, this misunderstanding has never been addressed.

Since everything that comes from the small self is opposite to that which is eternal and real, it naturally carries within itself a sense of vulnerability, further strengthening our innate fear. But fear serves only fear; it has no other purpose. Since it is at the root of the belief in separation, it is a powerful drug-like force that prevents us from experiencing life from higher levels of consciousness. This is why those who desire to control individuals or entire populations will use fear. It is the most powerful weapon. Given this innate fear for its survival, the ego is constantly engaged in battle, whether inner or outer. It must win those battles in order to hold our attention in the illusory state of separation. In recent years, as more and more members of the human collective are stirring and considering awakening as a very real possibility, we are seeing an increase in fear-inducing drama in the world.

But here is the greatest revelation of all: The small self only exists because it believes it has won the battle, and the only battle it can win is for our attention. What the ego fears the most is the moment you wake up and realize: Hey, that's not the real me, that's not all of what I am. I'm so much more than this measly small self! The ego's greatest opponent is you, choosing to come from your true Self. The ego can never derive satisfaction from this battle since the true Self does not fight, compete or engage in any form of battle. One who is aligned with the true Self does not know fear, for fear is only a product of the belief in separation.

The real threat to the small self is the fact that our awakening is available to us at any moment, despite its creative efforts to generate distracting drama. In this awakening, we are learning that we only appear to have needs since we only appear to have successfully disconnected from our Source. As expressions of the whole, infinite Source of Life, our only need is to remain connected to Source. Once connected, needs are met, and so they cease to exist. Once connected, lack and fear cease to exist. Once connected, we naturally tap into the infinite abundance of our Mother/Father Creator/Source.

From the limited perspective of the ego level of consciousness, this may appear as a boring, unexciting journey, certainly one that is not very validating for the small self. Who wants to have everything simply handed to you? I like working and fighting for what I want. I enjoy winning my battles! It makes me feel good; I'm good at it; it's exciting.

Yet, we are always free to choose: Which voice will we listen to today?

CHAPTER 7 • AN ISLAND ADVENTURE

The Connection That Matters

It was late January 2021, and I was deep into the writing of this book. Connected with inner guidance, I was uncovering new learning, exploring topics that had meaning for me, and so I was in a lush and peaceful place. Early one morning, I had a hunch to go to my website, probably based on a comment someone had made a week earlier. The reference on my homepage to my New Year numerology workshop needed to be updated from 2020 to 2021. Minor detail; it would only take a minute. After breakfast, hot cup of tea nearby, I went to log in to my website, but there was no website; it had disappeared.

After several calls to my web hosting provider, I learned that my domain name had expired the day before due to a technical error. This was a serious panic-worthy problem since my primary email address was based on this domain, which led me to spend hours replacing it with a functional one in dozens of online accounts. To give you an idea of what that might feel like, imagine having no smartphone or Internet access for a week—make that a month.

In just under two days, the domain name had been reactivated, and my email was functioning. I was free to return to writing. However, I wasn't really free. It wasn't enough to say, "It's all good, everything's fixed." I had lost something far more valuable than the connection to my website. I had lost the connection to my inner Self. I had experienced hell.

It then occurred to me that with a little patience and trust, instead of falling into fear and panic, I could have resolved these technical issues without losing my precious inner connection. Instead, I had set aside trust and opted for fear, a seemingly understandable reaction given the circumstance, right? But, as I learned first-hand, to be in fear is to be in hell. Fear is hell because where there is fear, God is not. To be disconnected from Source or separate from God is to be in hell.

Fortunately, since fear is a choice, and it is not of Source, it can simply be released. In order to reconnect, I engaged in those activities that brought me peace and joy. I went for a walk, fed the ducks and then headed for the kitchen, where I created a new muffin recipe while listening to an uplifting audiobook. At one point in the day, I caught a dose of healing medicine from Massenet's heavenly "Meditation" from Thais. Slowly but surely, the connection to Source was re-established.

That dark detour into hell had been based on the belief that my "survival" depended on the proper functioning of some technology. I had temporarily forgotten that my true survival depended on being connected to God/Source since this is the only connection that matters. For, where did I get that hunch to check my website the day after the domain had expired in the first place? From Source, of course.

> You may call upon a higher Intelligence, the higher Self of you, at any time, because it is not separate from you. It is accessible, has to be, because it is you. You may call upon that for guidance as to what to do, where to go, what to read, what to say. (Jeshua Online—Daily Message)

CHAPTER 8

Homeward Bound

[I]f you want to have a different experience of your world, you need to create a different experience of yourself. Be aware of which aspect of yourself you are using to create your reality, and through that awareness you will most certainly choose wisely. (*Ascension: The Shift to the Fifth Dimension*, Vol. 1, p. 56)

No Turning Back

For most of us, there is no doubt that the world in which we live could be better and, very likely, we don't want to live this way anymore, at least not without seeing significant improvement. It's also true that we want more, and we're curious to discover what this "more" might be like. We're ready to abandon some of our old beliefs and habits—maybe not all, though, not all at once, anyway. There are, after all, some good things about us; we're not all bad, right? We're ready to accept responsibility for our choices, although that's a hard pill to swallow—actually, it's not one we really want to swallow. So it is that we hesitate a bit. While we want a greater experience, we're not quite ready to leave our tiny island adventure behind, even if it means maintaining a state of separation from the Source of our infinite potential a little while longer. Though not perfect, at least on the island we know what to expect and we can manage okay—mostly.

Other than what is being channelled through new teachings, awakening, ascension, enlightenment, higher consciousness, Christ Mind, or anything other than our familiar body/mind experience is something we know very little about. What is this Home, this fifth dimension or this Kingdom of Heaven we keep hearing about? Will we ascend and disappear into some vast, empty, unknown, soul-spirit, high-frequency, interdimensional, unliveable space? Oh, and what about the cost? Maybe there's a catch; maybe we should be careful. Maybe we're being lured into space slavery by dark forces or evil aliens. I'm not sure this consciousness pioneer business is a good idea. Besides, I'm not even sure I deserve that "more" that's being dangled in front of us. Maybe I don't need more; maybe I have enough. I can put up with life as it is now; it's not that bad.

Well, the thing is, giving up the journey now is not an option, as it is not going to work. The journey has begun, and the shift is underway. You can call it the transition from Pisces to Aquarius, an intergalactic vibrational shift, Armageddon, the resurrection, the great transfiguration or any other name. The fact is that creation is not set in stone, change is forever ongoing and it has always been in place. There is a significant shift occurring right now, and whether we like it or not, significant change is at hand and it has the potential to make all things new.

Furthermore, while it will be evidenced in the world around us, change will not be accomplished from without. Since we are all contributing members of this collective experience for humanity, change needs to occur within each individual. Over the past couple of thousand years—which is but a moment in time in the long history of humanity—that vise-grip has been tightening bit by bit, and now it's reached its limit. At some point, something breaks, and this is where humanity stands as we transition into the Age of Aquarius. We are at a breaking point. The pressure is on for us to release the old and explore something new, to make a choice for a way of being that is completely different. The greater the readiness for change, the greater the shift and the greater the experience for all.

No doubt everyone has noticed the increase in drama in our movies, books, television shows and all manner of gaming and entertainment industries. We are a long way off from *Father Knows Best*, a popular, low-drama television show when I was growing up,

CHAPTER 8 • HOMEWARD BOUND

or *Sesame Street*, the show I watched with my daughters when they were young. As far as the news media are concerned, it has become nearly impossible to distinguish the "noise" from the facts. The old expression, "if it bleeds, it leads" has morphed into "let it bleed."

This heightened drama in our world is, in part, a low consciousness ego attempt to address the collective call for more and has been easy to implement during the drama-inclined Pisces Era. This response to our call has been further facilitated with the rise of the information technologies that have emerged thanks to the added energies of Aquarius. We are asking for more, and we are beginning to claim more of what we are but, without a shift in consciousness, our call is being answered with nothing more than an amplified version of the old. And so the ego, or small self, eagerly steps in and gives us more in the only form it can provide—unbridled drama, fear, emotionality, divisiveness, self-denial—all the while distracting us from reaching up for the more that awaits in our higher level of consciousness.

In a sense, the bad times or challenging, tragic and dramatic events encountered in the human condition are sort of a crapshoot for the ego since they can go either way. On the one hand, bad times are likely to keep our attention focused on the world. Distracted by fear, anxiety and worry, away from the quiet centre within, it is difficult to access the wisdom of the true Self—a win for the ego.

On the other hand, the challenging times, as have been experienced in recent years, can just as easily cause us to turn around and seek something else instead, hence the influx of new teachings and updates to traditional teachings that address our desire for awakening—our desire for another way of being. The bad times can then be turned into wonderful learning opportunities, thereby facilitating our rise to higher levels of consciousness. For many on the planet at this time, if it wasn't for the tough times, they may never have asked for another way, nor would we be experiencing the current trend of expanding awareness, a trend that is rapidly growing within the human collective.

While there may be more and more individuals expressing the need for significant change for themselves, for humanity and for planet Earth, there are those who are not ready for change. These individuals are choosing to remain firmly aligned with the low consciousness of the small self, and they will resist the invitation to rise above and beyond the separation experience. Not ready to embrace the changes required for a smooth transition to the new level of consciousness, or perhaps not wanting to disrupt their comfortable lifestyle, they will object to this growing movement. To delay the shift, they may even add to the drama by promoting fear, and as fear serves only fear, they may easily accomplish their goal. Don't be ridiculous. There's no proof that these teachings are real. Consciousness pioneers—really? You're being lured into a trap so "they" can have power over you. However, those who resist the shift do not realize that they are being controlled by their own fear of change, the result of clinging to the ego, the lower consciousness self. And so, because we choose to be from a higher level of consciousness, we let them be and simply love them.

It is true that through good times and bad times, we have enjoyed playing and learning and growing on our little island of separation. But now, increasingly weary, many are looking far off shore and wondering what lies beyond the body/mind experience. We cannot continue in this downward, tightening spiral. Because we are ready, we are now actively seeking to learn how to rise above the limited level of consciousness of the small self to the much higher level of the true Self. In our expanding state of consciousness, outdated, traditional, limiting beliefs are being released, making room for new learning. From the perspective of the true Self, we will no longer be limited to the body/mind sphere and will then be able to integrate higher knowledge into our experience.

We can argue and debate the meaning of the messages brought forth in these new teachings until kingdom come, especially considering that some of them are pretty far out. Messages from space beings? Jesus? Arcturians? Archangels? God? This kind of debate will be common in the science-minded, atheistic, non-religious climate

CHAPTER 8 · HOMEWARD BOUND

of Aquarius, but it will lead us nowhere. Remember duality—that less-than-enlightened trait we perfected during our experiment in separation from Source? The "I'm right, you're wrong" scuffle is part of the dualistic mindset we are leaving behind—or at least trying to.

While science is rapidly catching up with those in search of a shift in consciousness, it will take time before sufficient proof is provided, if proof is at all possible. Keeping in mind that the tools of the day have been developed to serve the current level of consciousness, in time, as we attain higher levels of consciousness, new tools will be developed. Meanwhile, for those who are eager to explore what lies ahead, we can skip over the lack of scientific proof and explore those new teachings that appeal to us.

All life experiences serve to direct our attention to where the truth lies—right in the centre of our Being. Ultimately, the teacher is found within, while the classroom is found in the everyday world. As we apply what we are learning, first-hand experience leads to the knowledge that has meaning for us, knowledge that enhances our journey. In this way, we are being encouraged to claim our sovereignty, to use our inner Christ discernment, to rely on our higher Self.

Individual sovereignty may be seen as contrary to certain traditional teachings and belief systems, as it removes the need for group or collective control measures. A person who is plugged into the wisdom of the higher Self is not likely to submit themselves to the rule of external forces. On the other hand, sovereignty is a very attractive attribute in the Aquarius climate of independence and self-reliance. However, there is a difference between true Self sovereignty and ego-based self-centred, independent wilfulness. The idea is to find the balance point of who and what we are as unique expressions of Source in a position of service for All.

As we transition into this new Aquarian climate, many are having little glimpses of what might be in store for humanity—a world of equality, abundance, community and inclusiveness, a readiness to care for all life on Earth. The choices we make during this transition period will establish the foundation of our future collective experience on the planet we claim as our home. What will we choose? Will we follow the glimmer of light that is inviting us to experience full conscious awareness, awakening? Or will we become experts at locking ourselves down out of fear? Will we listen to the quiet inner voice of the true Self or the noisy, dramatic clamouring of the small self, the ego? Awakening will be the result of our sincere desire to experience the more of what we are and, since we are creator beings, the means for our awakening will come as we express the desire.

Ubuntu

The following story has been circulating the web for some time now. While I could not find a reference to its origin, I thought I would share it here, reworded slightly because, well, that's what writers do. Its message truly embodies the heart and spirit of the higher level of consciousness of Aquarius, the level we are seeking to attain at this time of transition.

An anthropologist invited a group of children of an African tribe to play a game. He placed a basket full of fresh fruits at the foot of a tree. He then said, "The first child to reach the tree will get the whole basket." He clapped his hands and said, "Go!" To his great surprise, instead of rushing out toward the tree, the children smiled, came together, held hands and headed for the basket until they reached the tree where they shared the fruit.

"Why did you head out together when one of you could have gotten the basket of fruit all to yourself?" he asked.

Now it was the children who were startled, for, to them, the answer was obvious. "Ubuntu. How can one of us be happy while the rest are not?"

Ubuntu is a South African term for community, oneness and unity. I am because we are. How very Aquarian!

CHAPTER 8 • HOMEWARD BOUND

Learning to Trust the Feeling

One of the best gauges for making choices—though it may not seem rational or reasonable or scientific—is a much undervalued skill: the ability to feel. Did you feel that story about Ubuntu? You must have. Despite the fundamentally intellectual, scientific character of Aquarius, it does carry a deep sensitivity—perhaps even a vulnerability—to feeling. There comes a time when too much drama does not feel good. With my Moon in Aquarius, I know this all too well; I even fast-forward through dramatic scenes in Hallmark Movies. This sensitivity may actually be a beneficial trait during this transition period, as low tolerance for excessive drama will demand that emotionality be set aside so that logical, intelligent choices can be made instead. However, in our eagerness to bring about radical change, we should not completely abandon the ability to feel. If that were possible, then we would be lowering our consciousness even further, to the level of robots, and then perhaps one day we would become expendable crew members.

We have all used feelings to determine decisions, actions and choices. Everyone has had moments when they felt good, they were centred and peaceful and, in that state, made what turned out to be good choices, even great decisions. I took this job because it just felt right, and it turned out to be the best decision ever! I just had a feeling it was time to move on, no reason, just a feeling, and it was the right thing to do. These choices make us feel joyful and never leave us in doubt or uncertainty.

On the other hand, everyone knows what it's like to make a decision when feeling out of balance, emotional, fearful, angry, defiant, arrogant, in other words, not connected with the true Self. I was angry, I lost control. It's going to cost me a fortune to fix the car! I was so crazy about him, I couldn't say no. I should have listened to that niggling feeling that there was something wrong. He never told me he was married! These choices may bring feelings of regret, anger and self-recrimination. However, whether we see them as positive or negative, all experiences remain learning opportunities.

Fortunately, we came into being with an inner guidance system, a communication device that is permanently connected to our higher Self, which in turn has never stopped being connected to Source. Once again, the fact that we have this reliable, built-in gauge—an inner GPS—to help guide us in the right direction is proof that there is more to us than we realize. More often than not, this inner GPS speaks to us through feeling, the one attribute that may provide all that is needed for knowing in a given situation. It's not logical, it's not scientific, it's not the result of seven hours of research, debate, pondering and analysis, it's not fancy—it's just a feeling. Never underestimate the power of feeling, for it has the capacity to connect you with the meaning and experience and learning that has significance for you in the moment.

The tendency, especially among seekers, is to look for answers in books or teachings. You can spout out fancy words from holy books or the works of learned scientists and teachers—all potentially meaningful words—but if you're not feeling the words, they are most likely meaningless and without true impact for you—at least at the moment. Perhaps one day these words will trigger a feeling, an overwhelming aha moment, at which point they will be meaningful. Until that time, it is entirely appropriate to seek out, and even mix and match, those teachings and words and practices that have meaning for you now. You will immediately recognize these, for they will be accompanied by a good feeling. As you grow accustomed to making use of your inner GPS, as you remember to connect with your higher, divine Self, it becomes easier to discern what is and what is not appropriate for you in any given situation.

When talking to clients about feelings, I am reminded of the scene in the movie *Get On Up* where James Brown, played by Chadwick Boseman, attempts to share with his band members—professionally trained musicians—how he wants them to play the beat in a particular song. They immediately argue that it doesn't make sense musically. Growing frustrated because they don't get what he is trying to convey, finally, he says, "Does it sound good? Does it feel good? God made your ears. You didn't make 'em. You

CHAPTER 8 · HOMEWARD BOUND

don't argue with God's ears. If it sounds good and it feels good, then it's musical. So play it like I say play it. From the top. One, two, one, two, hit it." Then, all of a sudden, they get it, they feel it and they break out in an awesome, funky "Cold Sweat." Maybe this isn't the most peace-inducing piece of music, but it has soul! Also, it's a great song to loosen up with after having spent five hours at the computer. Gotta shake out those shoulders! Who said pioneering couldn't be fun. Okay, back to work.

Speaking of the Godfather of Soul, several years ago, while walking downtown one summer afternoon during the Montreal Jazz Festival, a group of young musicians were performing "It's A Man's Man's Man's World." What caught my attention was that they had switched up the words to sing "it's a woman's world." I found these young men—perhaps in their early twenties—to be rather bold, and I loved them for that boldness. We are truly living in changing times!

As we learn to value our inner GPS and listen to and trust our feelings, answers and insights will emerge. The question is, how do you feel about the idea of experiencing an ever-expanding state of consciousness, one that can encompass so much more than what you are experiencing now? How do you feel about the idea that you are more than a physical body, that you are mind, spirit, light, energy, soul, and that you can create so much more than what you have been creating up until now?

Boring!

One of the primary functions of drama, especially fear, is to validate the small self's need for self-protection, a need that is founded on the belief in separation from Source. The ego, the lower consciousness self, has a very important job—or so it wants you to believe. It derives and maintains its sense of power and authority by channelling energy into self-protection, competition, acquiring material goods and the struggle for survival. The absence of drama will thereby appear unworthy of the ego's attention. It needs and seeks stimulation in the form of challenges and excitement, as these lower states of consciousness keep it alive. From the ego's perspective, peace is boring. It might be said that the ego's GPS is drama. The louder the message, the greater the life experience and the more significant and empowered is the small self. Bring it on!

Another important function of drama, perhaps even its primary function, is to keep the state of peace at bay. The ego creates and feeds drama in order to keep us from experiencing peace since its very existence is based on the opposite of peace. Among the most powerful and effective tools at our disposal for facilitating awakening to the full experience and expression of our true Being is peace. As *A Course in Miracles* states, peace is the condition for passing through that doorway to Source. If we are unable to experience peace, we will be unable to rise above the lower level of consciousness of the separated self. The ego's status as director of our life thus remains intact. To set aside the drama and say yes to peace is to shut down the ego's main avenue of communication and control. To the ego, peace is dangerous—peace is to the ego what kryptonite is to Superman.

> The distraction of the ego seems to interfere with your learning, but the ego HAS no power to distract you, unless you GIVE it the power. (ACIM, Ch. 8, p. 173)

The Choice for Peace

All my clients claim that they want peace. However, when we explore those difficult situations for which they seek resolution—and peace—it becomes clear that the peace they desire comes with conditions. Desire that comes with predetermined conditions is not likely to come from our higher Self. If only he would stop yelling; if only they took my opinions seriously; if only they would clean up their rooms; if only my boss weren't such a jerk; if only the economy were better; if only my health improved; if only I had more money; if only we had better schools; if only my candidate were elected; if only… if only… if only… I would be at peace. Under these conditions, true peace will not be found. If being from peace depended on external circumstances, there would be no hope. In order to have

CHAPTER 8 · HOMEWARD BOUND

peace, it must come from within; it is the result of a choice only we can make, and like true love, peace is unconditional.

Peace is essential to making the connection with the higher Self. This blessed connection then allows us to experience the infinite love, comfort and support that come from our Creator/Source, God. When we connect with the higher Self, the ego no longer has a place in our awareness since noise is not acknowledged, nor has it any power, in the state of peace. In that peaceful state, the ego has lost its job. It is while being in a peaceful state that we can cross the threshold and experience the overwhelmingly blissful feeling of our higher consciousness. Peace opens the door to possibilities beyond the known, for in peace, there is no fear, no drama and no overwhelming emotionality. There are only wholeness, joy and infinite possibilities.

Since it is a simple matter of choice, peace is available at any moment. All that is needed is to want peace more than the fear, drama, pain or suffering that was being experienced. What is being experienced is always the consequence of a choice made in response to an invitation either from the ego or from the higher Self. Once we become aware that we have accepted the wrong invitation, a correction is in order. It is then entirely appropriate to say "no" to the invitation of the small self, as this is an innate power that can never be taken away from us.

When the small self, or ego, intrudes in your awareness with a distraction that may upset your peace, simply say no. Don't be afraid; no one will even know what you are doing. Simply call on that inner Self, and say no. As you begin to experience the benefits and joy of that powerful connection with the true Self, you will increasingly desire peace above all else, the peace that is beyond understanding and is deeply felt.

In the Ubuntu story, the children had the wisdom to pause a moment and check in with their inner wisdom. This put them in the best state of consciousness to make a decision as to how they would claim the wonderful gift of the basket of fruit. In that quiet moment of peace, they knew—and no doubt felt—the love of their oneness. Together, they knew that sharing the gift was far greater than claiming it for themselves.

The Quiet Mind

I shared an exercise in *Choosing the Miracle*, but I am not aware of anyone ever having tried it. It was basically a simple, three-hour practice of being in silence, disconnected from the outside world. No breathing, mantras or poses; nothing complicated or fancy. Throughout my youth, I spent many weekends, even weeks, in silent retreats, enjoying the peaceful tranquillity of many local and surrounding monasteries. I know, weird, but that was my journey. Of course, this was in the days before tablets and smartphones—we didn't even have cable TV—so I never gave a second thought to the "three-hour" aspect of the exercise. What's three hours, right? Well, it seems that three hours of silence today is like three months fifty years ago. So, in this modified version, feel free to substitute the amount of time you would like to set aside. Try at least thirty minutes; maybe twenty; fifteen? It shows first-hand how difficult it is to break away from the addictive noisy clutches of the small self, even if we are sincere in our desire to connect with the true Self.

Pick an evening or any time of day when you have no obligations, when you will have some quiet time for yourself. Turn off all the noise and potential sources of distraction: phones, television, tablets, computer. Put a Do Not Disturb sign on your door. Don't post your intention on your social media page; don't text your BFF. Be uncompromising; this is your moment. Have a simple, light meal, no stimulants, no coffee or alcohol—nothing you might blame for feeling uncomfortable, anxious or restless, or for falling asleep.

Since the experience of full conscious awareness is not found outside but rather inside, here is an opportunity to journey there. Set yourself up in a quiet room, in a comfortable chair or lying down with pillows underneath your knees, head and lower back as you might do in a Restorative Yoga pose. Have a blanket nearby, in case you feel cold, which is common when relaxing into a quiet meditative state. Once comfortably settled, begin to take long, slow, deep

CHAPTER 8 · HOMEWARD BOUND

breaths. You may find that simply releasing yourself into this experience of peacefulness naturally causes you to take very deep, wide breaths. Breathing is our connection with Life and so consciously taking deep breaths connects us with Source. As the barriers to this connection with Source are dropped, as the idea of separation is released, experience expands.

Once you are feeling the peaceful flow of Life infusing all levels of your awareness, you can vary the breath by breathing in Love, God, Source or healing energy, anything you feel you need to bring into your life. You can then breathe out illness, stress, worrying thoughts, sadness, memories or anxiety—anything you wish to release. If you are feeling peaceful and are currently not disturbed by anything that needs releasing, you may breathe out something you wish to share with the world around you, such as harmony, community spirit, healing, peace and light. This practice can be used anytime during the day, whenever there is a feeling of being uncentred or not plugged into your true Self, or simply for the soothing feeling of peace it provides. Try it while stopped at a red light in your car, while washing the dishes or while out walking the dog.

Try not to use this time to think. You can think about your master's thesis or your career-defining sales pitch after the exercise. You may find that after having experienced deep peace, you are more inspired, and this will translate into a brilliant thesis or an awesome sales pitch. Remember, if you're thinking, you're probably not feeling—at least not the inspired feelings that arise out of peace and that divine inner connection. Turn off the thinking apparatus, let go and fall into the arms of eternal, infinite, living Love. Love feels so good. Actually, there are no suitable words to describe the feeling of being surrounded and filled by Love—there is only the experience. Seek only the experience.

If you are bold enough to try the full three-hour version, take occasional walks around the room or the house, in silence, as needed, to remain alert. Remember: no television, no phone, no computer; do not check your text messages, do not post your status on social media. Only quiet. Do not judge yourself if you were unable to remain in your quiet space for the full amount of time allotted. Keep in mind that you chose the amount of time you wanted for the exercise; you can always try a shorter amount at a later date. This exercise is meant as a way of becoming aware of the degree to which we resist the peaceful silence; it is not an invitation to engage in the monastic life.

After your first experience, a next step might be to sit quietly for five-minute periods, perhaps two or three times a day. With repeated practice, the quiet mind is nurtured and strengthened. As the desire to experience a peaceful mind grows, the ability to sit, walk and stand in quiet stillness grows. As we become more and more familiar with this peaceful state, it becomes possible to recall this quiet stillness while driving the car, at work or out shopping for groceries. As an invaluable benefit, you will find through direct experience that you are making wiser and more enlightened choices and decisions in your everyday life. You may also find yourself in a better position to help your brothers and sisters. This sense of peace and wholeness becomes a normal and even sought-after activity, just like eating, drinking or even breathing.

Once you have become comfortable with this experience of quiet peacefulness, you can modify it slightly so that while taking in and releasing deep breaths you allow yourself to be completely infused with Creator/Source, God. Let all of your physicality be released as you rise above your lower consciousness body/mind state to your higher, more subtle, spiritual level of Being. As you rise to the higher level of consciousness, every cell of your body, every aspect of your being becomes spirit, light, energy and love. Take the time to feel it. It feels so good.

If you think that three hours or even thirty minutes of quiet time is long, I will share this story. Many years ago, maybe forty-five years, in a metaphysical group, we were asked to do a four-hour immobility exercise. This was a four-hour session of conscious, absolute immobility, without even batting an eyelash, and was more like a trial of endurance. So as requested, I lay down on the floor on

CHAPTER 8 • HOMEWARD BOUND

my back, closed my eyes, and remained in total immobility. I don't quite recall the details of the event, but I think a supervisor was informing us of the time elapsed throughout the exercise.

Somehow, just past the three-hour mark, I became a tiny bit restless. I had not batted an eyelash or even twitched a single muscle in all that time. However, I became curious to know what it would feel like to move a muscle, and so I ever so slightly tightened a muscle in my lower back. Since there had been no outward sign of movement, it was deemed that I had successfully completed the trial. But I knew better, so when we had the opportunity to do it a second time a few months later, I was pleased to complete the trial without a single twitch. What did I learn from this little experiment? That I could lie in perfect immobility for four hours? Nope. I learned that I could not lie to myself and, in the end, that's all that mattered.

For those who sincerely desire to make that connection with their higher Self, the quiet mind soon becomes a welcome and preferred alternative to the noisiness of the world with which we are familiar. If meditation is too difficult, it is possible to find other, even creative, means to cajole the mind into quietness. Walking in the woods, listening to soothing music (though probably not "Cold Sweat"; save that for exercise time), sitting by a gently flowing stream, working in the garden, taking your dog for a walk, completing a jigsaw puzzle, painting, soaking in a hot bath, watching snowflakes swirl to the ground, baking bread, playing a musical instrument, woodworking, quilting, following a butterfly as it flutters from branch to branch—there are countless activities that can help foster an experience of quietness. Including more of those quiet, peaceful activities in daily life nurtures the desire for the shift in consciousness.

Another wonderful time to put this into practice is after you lay your head down on the pillow at night. As you prepare for sleep, recall this feeling of peacefulness. Breathe deeply, and connect with your true Self, the portal to Creator/Source, God. Let go of any memories of the day, any thoughts of tomorrow, and just be in the moment. Breathe. Now, let yourself fall into the arms of the loving

God, Mother/Father, Abba, Creator/Source, whatever language allows you to feel the Love that is the Source of Life. Imagine falling through space and time, surrounded by Love. Now consciously love yourself. Breathe. Let go. Let Love infuse every aspect of your body, mind and soul.

Embracing the Chooser

Don't feel bad if you weren't able to sit through your allotted time for the previous exercise. You can do it again another day. In fact, you should never feel bad about anything since everything you experience—the good and the bad—is the result of a choice made by you and is thus always an opportunity for learning. Try this: See that cup of coffee or glass of water next to you where you're sitting and reading? If you don't have one, go get one. Now, look at that glass or cup and knock it over. Yes, you read correctly. Knock it over.

Okay, what do you have now? If you did as instructed, you probably have a mess to clean up—a small mess, not as bad as some of the big ones in your life. Maybe you feel annoyed for having done so. What a stupid thing to do! You may even blame the stupid author of this dumb book for suggesting that you do that in the first place. Yet, you *chose* to follow instructions. Remember, you have the power. You may ask yourself why you did as instructed, at which point, you realize that you are accustomed to following instructions without checking in with your higher Self. Or, maybe you were just curious and acted on impulse. Lesson learned.

Perhaps you chose not to do as instructed. This is dumb. No one is going to tell me what to do! If you didn't tip over that cup of coffee, you're probably pleased with yourself for not having fallen for that lame trick. In this case, what was the learning opportunity? That you can successfully defy authority? Did you remember to breathe deeply and connect with your higher Self before making that choice?

Or, maybe you did take a moment for that deep breath before deciding what to do. Having gained access to inner wisdom, you instantly knew the meaning of the exercise: you remembered that you always have the power and the freedom to choose. Connected with your higher Self, you naturally felt love for yourself for having created an opportunity to remember who and what you are. Filled with that love, you smiled and maybe took another deep breath. Feeling grateful, you took a sip of the water and were reminded that you are a beloved expression of the Ocean of Life. You learned through first-hand experience that taking that moment to check in with true Self pays off!

Whatever the outcome, a choice was made, and that's good news because it shows that we always have the freedom to choose our experience. Freedom of choice is a wonderful gift, and as powerful creator beings, our choices will naturally have consequences. Be grateful for this great gift. Every choice made and every action taken then becomes a learning opportunity. We may choose appropriately or inappropriately, but it is a choice nonetheless, and this freedom is a highly valued aspect of Aquarius.

By our choices, we create our experiences and opportunities. These choices are also reflected in our interactions with others and in our world. Since our actions are the result of our freedom to choose, there is never any reason to feel "bad" for anything we have done. We make choices based on the level of consciousness with which we are aligned at the moment. If we have not taken that quiet moment to breathe and connect with the higher Self, our choices are likely to be based on emotional responses, reactions, beliefs, learning, memories and past experience acquired while in alignment with the small self, or ego. It is then possible to choose to align differently in the next moment. We are always free to choose to disconnect from the ego and to connect with our higher Self at any moment of the day, under any situation and given any circumstance. Being aware of this will greatly enhance and facilitate our shift in consciousness.

Look back over your day and examine some of the choices you made. Where did these choices come from? In the same way, you can look back over your life and re-examine some of the choices you made, but this time, from a different perspective, without judgment or condemnation. What did you learn from these choices? The point is to keep in mind that we always chose freely.

Knowing that you always choose freely, you cannot say, "The ego made me do it" or "He is such an ego." The ego is simply a lower level of consciousness; it is not who you truly are. Your thoughts, actions and words are you in manifestation, you in expression. You are free to choose which aspect of yourself you will express and manifest: either the lower consciousness small self or the higher consciousness divine Self. There is a chooser, and it is the chooser we must look at, embrace, educate and love.

> The failure of outer things to satisfy leads the soul to seek the power within. Then the individual may discover that I AM, he may know that within him lies all power to satisfy the soul, to fulfill its every need and desire. This knowledge may not come until the individual is driven by the buffetings of the world to seek this inner plane of peace and calm. (*Life and Teachings of the Masters of the Far East*, Vol. 1, p. 143)

CHAPTER 9

Awakening to Oneness

> You make choices and you live with the effects of those choices, but they are all part of your journey. It is the divine journey of awakening, and you have never made a wrong choice.... You are making your reality every moment. That is how powerful you are. (*Jeshua: The Personal Christ*, Vol. VII, p. 145)

The Journey of Life

This journey of awakening to the experience of who and what we truly are seems rather long. What if some are tired and don't want to journey anymore? We've been around the block many, many times, and we want to experience something new, something easier, something completely different. But, do we really need this long and difficult journey? Haven't we had enough? Does it ever end? Although fewer in number over the past couple of years, there are those who are having a great time and want to continue their journey. They may be at the top of the world or still making their way up but, for them, there is so much more to be experienced. Life is exciting and, above all, self-gratifying. They don't want to change anything.

Whether or not we like it, we are always on a journey. Life is a journey since all life is the expression of the Creative Life Principle, and the Creative Life Principle is forever in motion, unfolding, expressing, expanding and being. That is the very nature of life, and so life on planet Earth has always been experiencing growth, expansion and change. You can call it the "times," the new Era, the shift in consciousness, the higher vibration, a galactic transition, a new season—call it whatever you like, there is no getting around the fact that change is afoot because change is a natural aspect of life. What matters is how ready we are to accept it and, as creator beings with a significant role to play, how we can implement these changes for the good of all life on Earth.

For thousands and thousands of years, our journeys have been focused on experimenting and playing as autonomous, independent body/mind beings functioning as though we were separate from Source, or independent from the Creative Life Principle. We have learned and accomplished much during our time in the human condition on planet Earth but, in our eagerness to explore and make the most of our experience, we have forgotten a few key points about who and what we are. Whether or not we are ready to accept that we are creator beings and as such we are responsible for our lives and our world, memory is returning and deep, inner knowing is rising to our awareness. And so it makes sense that more and more brothers and sisters are beginning to realize that we deserve something else, something more than what this journey has brought us thus far.

That we have not completely forgotten that there is more to us than the 3-D level of experience is evidenced by our nearly constant search for more, whether it is for a better quality of life, a better job, a bigger house or simply more joy. Up until now, we have generally sought to fulfill this longing within the context of our current level of consciousness. This means that the desire for an experience that lies beyond the known must come from another aspect of us; it must come from the higher Self, the true Self. It is this aspect of ourselves that we must connect with and fully embrace, as it is the essential driving force behind who and what we are.

No matter how tired we are, rather than seeking to end the journey, perhaps we can use our newly expanding consciousness to make a few corrections—okay, maybe a lot of corrections. Looking back on the journey of the human collective as well as on our own individual journeys, we are opening our eyes and seeing that, without a doubt, change is needed. For those who are having a great life and are not keen on changing anything, imagine if that life could be one hundred times better. For those who have experienced struggle, lack or difficulty of any kind, imagine a completely different life, without struggle, lack or difficulty. Since we are beginning to explore the fact that we are essentially powerful creator beings, anything is possible.

During this transition phase where old structures are being dismantled and new ones are emerging, we can explore an entirely new journey—one that will be completely different from what we have known for so long, one that will bring joy, wonder, peace, abundance and fulfillment for all beings on Earth. Since we are curious to experience more of who and what we are, and since curiosity is an innate trait of Aquarius, all that needs to be considered is how can we ease into this major transition for ourselves and for all of humanity.

Shedding Light on Oneness

Before moving forward with our journey and before further exploring what this time of shift will mean for us, it may be helpful to examine one subject that could be considered a bit of a thorn as we transition into the independent and autonomous climate of Aquarius, and that is the subject of "Oneness." Among the greatest challenges or hurdles we will face during this time of shift will be the fear of losing our hard-earned freedoms, independence, autonomy and individuality. We have fought long and hard for these great gifts over the past few hundred years, and we are not willing to give them up. Besides, there is still a long way to go before everyone on Earth is enjoying the same freedoms, and we don't want to break the momentum. While the climate of Aquarius supports the spirit of community, it will not be implemented at the cost of individual freedoms. So, what does Oneness really mean? What will be the cost? Will we lose our uniqueness and our precious freedoms?

These concerns are understandable given that the human condition as we currently know and experience it is deeply rooted in the belief in separation, an unnatural condition that must be cultivated, protected and maintained. If it were natural, it would simply flow with ease, harmony, abundance and without the need for competition, strain or struggle. As creator beings endowed with the gift of freedom of choice, we, together, have agreed to maintain this state of separation. Other than our long-held beliefs, there is nothing outside of us forcing us to maintain this agreement. And so it will be maintained until we decide otherwise.

Since separation is the state with which we are most familiar at this time, there may be hesitation, resistance and fear at the thought of abandoning it for something as radical as Oneness, for something that could potentially take away our freedoms, for something we cannot recall ever having experienced. As we know, fear is a powerful motivator, and the separated self can, and will, use fear to trigger resistance to this experience of Oneness should it present a threat to its position as director of our lives.

The real question now is, has our state of separation from Source truly given us the freedom of expression we desire, the freedom to be who we truly are, the freedom to know our infinite potential? We are moving into a new Era that will require the release of that which is not in alignment with the new consciousness we are exploring. The transition from Pisces to Aquarius is like transferring the contents of a large glass of water into a medium-sized glass. The surplus from the large glass will overflow. In the same way, the surplus baggage from the previous Eras—the beliefs, behaviours and structures that are not in alignment with the energy of the new Era—simply will not fit.

Many are beginning to squirm under the pressures of the deeply rooted and ever-increasing control measures carried forward from the previous Eras. From the day we begin our journey on Earth, we are trained, educated and groomed to fit the mould of family, dogma, tradition, culture and community. We learn that in order to survive, we must conform to predetermined religious, societal, political and economic beliefs, rules and regulations. And so it is that from a very young age we learn to work the system and play

CHAPTER 9 • AWAKENING TO ONENESS

the game in the best way we can in order to meet our particular needs, goals and desires.

The effect of these programming measures is that they have established barriers, interfering with access to memory and awareness of what lies beyond the limits of the lower consciousness 3-D body/mind experience. Through this conditioning, we have effectively alienated ourselves from the truth of who and what we are as Source Energy beings of light, love and infinite creative potential. What we are now realizing is that all this time we have been depriving ourselves of our true, innate power as creator beings. Instead, we have been focusing on acquiring, gaining and maintaining power on the lowest level of experience possible.

Those few souls whose memory structures are stronger or who are not as susceptible to programming may retain a faint, lingering memory of the truth of their Being. These individuals often feel marginalized and have difficulty fitting into programmed societal structures. Some will be inspired to seek for truth through various spiritual and esoteric works, and are likely to be the ones finding solace in the new teachings being brought to us at this time of transition. A few will find escape in a fantasy world of their own making, thereby never really connecting with what is commonly defined as "reality." They are likely to be labelled as suffering from some form of psychological disorder. Others will attempt to escape the uncomfortable trappings of the lower consciousness human condition in less enlightened and, at times, less healthy ways. With Neptune energies in the mix over the past 2000 years, we have seen escapism rise to a whole new level, including everything from overwork to abuse of alcohol and drugs as well as countless forms of distracting media, games and so-called entertainment.

As we shift into the freedom-loving Era of Aquarius, a growing fear of loss of individuality and autonomy through the misuse and corruption of socio-economic power is emerging. Globalization of economic, social and cultural systems has developed naturally over the past couple of hundred years as we learned to travel, exchange and trade with others around the globe. How globalization will be used in the coming years will be determined by the inherent level of consciousness that will drive this movement forward. From a lower state of consciousness founded on the belief in separation, it is likely to be used to foster self-serving dystopian global controls. If globalization is guided by a higher level of consciousness, we will experience a shift toward freedom, fairness, abundance, humanitarianism, equality and a growing sense of community for and with all on Earth as well as throughout the galaxy and beyond. Again, the direction of our journey will depend on the choices we make today.

The concept of the Oneness of Creation/Reality has been at the heart of many ancient teachings and was recognized as the essence of our existence. It was reintroduced by Jesus at the start of the Pisces Era, the one climate that could most naturally nurture and sustain a consciousness of universal inclusiveness, Love and Unity. However, as beings in the human condition had long ago replaced Oneness with separation as the foundational principle of existence, so it is that the invitation made by Jesus was not quite well received. With a deeply ingrained belief in separation from Source, the long-standing culture of divisiveness was maintained and further developed throughout the Era of Pisces, a culture that has brought much needless suffering, lack and inequality for far too many on Earth.

Looking back, it seems as though Jesus was 2000 years ahead of his time. However, one can only imagine what life would be like today if he had not sowed that initial seed of Love and Unity, for, while it did not flourish to its full potential, it resides still in our hearts and souls. The consciousness of Love and Unity lies in waiting for the moment when we will acknowledge that it is the essence of our Being as expressions of Source Energy. Fortunately, we do not need to wait any longer, for the time to embrace and experience this higher consciousness is now. All that is needed is that we turn within and water that seed of Love and Unity, for it has never left our hearts.

CHAPTER 9 · AWAKENING TO ONENESS

The Shadow of Oneness

From the perspective of the ego sense of self, the idea of a harmonious Oneness might sound boring, even dangerous or threatening. During the Aries Era in particular, we learned to thrive and prosper in a challenging, competitive, survivalist climate. Combined with the desire to accumulate valuables and material goods as was enhanced during the Taurus Era, in time, alignment with the lower consciousness self provided a strong sense of worth, purpose and satisfaction. Through struggles, challenges, victories and conquests, the separated self emerged as a powerful force of its own. While in alignment with the small self, we came to believe that we can actually live quite well and flourish independently from Source Energy. This fact is evidenced by our overall beliefs about life as well as in the training and educational systems that promote competition, success at the cost of others, and the acquisition of material wealth as a sign of prosperity and success.

With separation from Source firmly established as our foundation, it was inevitable that divisiveness would permeate all levels of experience in the human condition. Over time, divisiveness became a normal feature of life on Earth, and so we learned to create firm, distinct boundaries between ourselves and others, around groups, cultures, societies and countries, effectively blocking out any possible experience of Oneness. This allowed a few to separate themselves out so as to be in a better position to control, manipulate and make decisions for the masses. Coming from a lower level of consciousness, the decisions made by those in control, or "in power," were more often than not made for their own benefit, to the detriment of the whole.

Throughout the age of Pisces, since our search for more came from a lower level of consciousness, we sought more and more drama, more divisiveness, more confusion and more emotion, all of which were lower expressions of the Era of Pisces. If we continue into Aquarius without raising our consciousness, this search for more will likely be expressed as more science, more confidence in what we think we know on the material, or lower, level of consciousness, or more freedom claimed by some individuals at the cost of the freedom of others. Hence a continued move away from Oneness, but now with the confidence and backing of science, information and data.

Fortunately, it is becoming increasingly difficult to ignore the fact that our little adventure into separation may not have been our best choice—at least not the most enlightened. We tried it, we played with it, but it doesn't represent the best of who and what we are as Source-based creator beings. Without knowing why, many are sensing that it doesn't feel quite right; something is off. This is because the idea of separation is fundamentally contrary to the principle of Oneness, an essential truth that has been withheld from most of our traditional teachings.

While there has been preaching about "the one God and the one heaven," for the most part we need to earn that place, behave in a certain way, adhere to selected beliefs and practices, or pay prescribed dues to even get close to this one God or to enter this heaven. Besides being separate from us, this God is not all-inclusive, He has "chosen ones," and so He cannot represent the Oneness we are now being invited to consider and reclaim as our natural condition. As we begin our journey in the Age of Aquarius, rigid, illogical, dogmatic belief systems are being replaced with common-sense perspectives and all-encompassing, holistic approaches to all aspects of life.

The idea of universal Unity or the One Source shared by all life is a prominent aspect of new teachings today. If we are to move forward to an experience of higher consciousness, Oneness will need to be considered, accepted and embraced. In Reality, or in the state of Oneness, duality cannot exist. The appeal of Oneness is growing as some are realizing that it is the only sane and intelligent alternative to divisiveness, which can only lead to struggle, war, senseless competition, suffering and inequality. Only the choice for divisiveness can cast a shadow. This is why many are hearing the call from within to return to the natural state of Oneness. This

CHAPTER 9 • AWAKENING TO ONENESS

call is an invitation from the inner voice, the true Self from which we have never been separated, the part of us that has always been nurtured and sustained in Oneness.

Fear may be experienced by those clinging to alignment with the ego, as divisiveness is the very foundation of the ego's existence. Oneness ensures the end of division and so will not be happily embraced by those who seek to maintain their experience of separation. In fact, the ego will fight against Oneness because its survival is based on separation. As Oneness is embraced, there will no longer be any need or desire for an ego sense of self, and so it will simply be released and eventually disappear from our experience.

Exercise: Releasing into Oneness

The next time you experience fear, confusion, sadness or any form of discomfort, try this exercise. If possible, find a quiet place where you will not be disturbed, perhaps go for a walk in nature or sit on a park bench. Take a couple of deep breaths. Remember that breathing is your direct line to Source Energy. Allow yourself to be filled with that soothing feeling of deep peace. Breathe deeply, filling those lungs to full capacity. Once your mind has become quiet, rise up and join with your higher Self, embrace your true Self. Breathe. Feel the warmth, the safety, the comfort and the strength of your true Self. Remember that your true Self remains always aligned with Source Energy, so this is a connection that can never be broken or taken away from you. When you are in alignment with your true Self, you know Oneness, and so you cannot possibly know fear or discomfort of any kind.

Now, from that place where you are joined with your higher Self, glance down at the troubling situation that made you feel fearful or uncomfortable. Breathe in Oneness, and as you breathe out, let it go. Let yourself be enveloped by the peace, joy, safety, warmth, Love and Unity of being joined with Oneness. Let that feeling sink in. This is what it feels like to be in alignment with your true Self.

As you return to your daily activities, you may be surprised to discover that a problem you had been trying hard to resolve now has a solution. Or an answer to a question that had been troubling you suddenly comes to mind, or a lost object magically appears out of nowhere. Perhaps, someone with whom you were finding it difficult to relate somehow has shifted their position and is now much easier to communicate with. You will find that as you function in alignment with Oneness, inspiration will naturally emerge when needed, and life will become easier. Throughout the day, remind yourself now and then to breathe deeply and rise up to your true Self. The more frequently you make this connection, the easier it becomes and the longer you can maintain this joyful, peaceful, creative, fulfilling state of consciousness. It would be foolish to turn down an opportunity to experience something that feels so good!

The Beauty and Power of Oneness

For some, the term Oneness may be much easier to work with than the word "God." However, if it can further set the Aquarian mind at ease, the term "Oneness" may be replaced with "Allness" or "Inclusiveness" or "Unity." Use any word that implies not only the natural innate solidarity, intelligence and cohesion of Life, but also its shared Source/Cause. As creator beings, we are always free to choose our experience, and so it's okay to create and use language, tools and means that facilitate our awakening to the more of what we are. We are beginning a new journey, and so we can make new choices.

Another misunderstanding of the idea of Oneness is that it means sameness, the annihilation of uniqueness or the loss of individuality and freedom. We incorrectly believe that our identity is founded on how we distinguish ourselves from each other in the world: our roles, how we look and dress, personality, social status, wealth, cultural identity, jobs, education and, especially, how we are perceived by others. We believe that if we unite as one family, we will lose our precious identities. This misunderstanding can only come from the small self, or ego, since it has a claim in the preservation of its position in separation. Since the ego can only make suggestions, the problem is easily solved. We can simply decline the

CHAPTER 9 • AWAKENING TO ONENESS

invitation to accept that it is possible to exist apart from Source/Creator/God and, instead, choose to explore our Oneness.

We have made significant advances over the past couple of hundred years on Earth, but we are still not living up to our full potential as intelligent, loving, caring, creator beings. If change is to be brought forth in the experience of the human collective, we must acknowledge that divisiveness is our weakness, our Achilles' heel. As creator beings, we have all the power needed to bring about change, but in a divided state, we have no true power. As long as identification with the separated small self is maintained, we only have the power to maintain an unnatural, dualistic condition.

At first, it may be difficult to comprehend the idea of a Oneness that encompasses all things, a Oneness that is being all things now and forever, to imagine a world in which everything is connected to everything else. We must first acknowledge that we have chosen this experience of separateness and that it is not being imposed on us. Every day, every minute of every day, we either choose to join with each other or we choose to attack, defend ourselves, push away or in some way be separate from each other.

The recognition of this truth is what will set us on the path to the journey home and the experience of the full conscious awareness of who we are as aspects of Source Energy, Oneness. The willingness to accept the idea that we are all connected will help release us from the idea of separation. Acceptance of the truth that there is a Source for all of Creation and that we are integral aspects of Creation will correct all errors and bring about the healing, wholeness and abundance we seek for ourselves and for all humankind.

Oneness is expressed in infinite ways and always in perfect harmony. The Source of Life is constantly being new and expressing Itself in every moment, always in a unique way. Incapable of conflict, it must exist in harmony otherwise it would damage or destroy Itself. If we are not experiencing freedom of expression, harmony, peace, wholeness and joy, if we are experiencing any form of limitation, conflict or "dis-ease," then we are not experiencing Oneness, or our full potential, and must therefore be in the state of separation. Since there are only two ways of being, it becomes easy to recognize which we have chosen.

If only Oneness exists and we are not experiencing Oneness then we are experiencing something that does not exist in Reality, or something that is not an expression of Creator/Source Energy. As is explained in some new teachings, what is being experienced instead of Reality is a dream, a cleverly made-up substitute for Reality, or an illusion. Note that the concept of dreams and illusions is in alignment with lower frequency Pisces and Neptune. Dreams and illusions can simply be brushed aside for what they are: nothing worthy of the attention of an awakening creator being.

A red rose will have variations in the shapes and colours of its petals, and it is these variations that give it its intrinsic beauty. If all the petals were of the same shape, size and colour, the flower would lose it uniqueness. If all the petals were pulled out, the rose would cease to be. In the same way, each being is unique and it is our differences that make the whole so wonderful. Even if we have adopted false beliefs about ourselves and followed rules and regulations that did not represent or support who we truly are, we have never lost and can never lose our essential uniqueness, or our authentic Self, as some like to call it. Since false beliefs are simply the result of mistaken choices, they can easily be abandoned. There is no need for judgment, condemnation or punishment. As we release that which does not reflect our uniqueness, our true Self will naturally emerge.

True freedom is liberation from the limiting beliefs that are inherent in the state of separation. As long as we continue to align with the separated self, we deny ourselves the opportunity to experience our wholeness, our complete freedom of Being. Freedom is experienced when illusion, ignorance and false conditioning are abandoned. The simple and easy remedy is to consciously choose to align with our true Self. Harmonious reunification with Source is the high consciousness attribute of the Pisces climate, a lesson we can now learn and integrate while we transition into the Age of Aquarius. Our inherent desire for freedom will inevitably lead us to welcome and embrace our higher Self.

CHAPTER 9 • AWAKENING TO ONENESS

Since it is not possible to be separate from Source, even as we know ourselves in the limited human condition, we have never stopped being living expressions of Oneness. Whatever we are doing, it is always from that place, albeit in a limited way. In our dualistic state of separation, we are not aware of the extent of our true power. Instead, what little power we have is misused to maintain an unnatural condition. We do not realize that the belief in separation is the cause of all of our problems, a situation that is easily remedied when we take the time to breathe and remember that we are a part of something far greater, that Oneness is our true condition. The truth is that we can't do anything without Creator/Source/God because Creator/Source/God is being all things at all times. As Jeshua taught: Of myself I can do nothing.

The Healing Power of Oneness

As recounted in *Making Peace with God,* when my youngest daughter Caroline was around six months old, she came down with what I immediately recognized as the symptoms of the croup. As the hours passed, her breathing grew more laboured, and her cough became increasingly raspy. Having been through this before with her older sister, I knew she would need to see a pediatrician for antibiotics. It was late, nearly midnight and everyone was fast asleep. While inhaling cold air was one of the remedies for croup, that night was far too cold to open a window. As she struggled more and more with each breath, I knew I had to do something. One thing was certain, I did not relish the thought of spending the night in the hospital emergency ward, and, if I waited until morning, I would have to make arrangements for a sitter for her sister.

With few appealing options available at the time, I decided to take matters in hand. Note that this occurred over forty years ago, long before I had a true understanding of Love and Unity. Clearly, on a deeper level, I knew something about the power of Oneness, a knowing we can all access. Sitting in the bentwood rocker with Caroline pressed gently against my breast, I closed my eyes and connected with my heart, that place from which emanated the deep love I felt for her. As we joined in Oneness, almost instantly, a warm energy began to flow from me into her tiny body. There was no questioning, no praying, not even any thinking or doubting. There was only the feeling—the feeling of love.

Then I said, sweetly and lovingly, but with the utmost conviction: "We don't need this." As I continued to rock her gently, I added, "We really don't." Bound by the simple warmth and wholeness of a mother's love for her child, we fell asleep in the rocker. The following morning, Caroline's symptoms had completely vanished. It had been a simple, normal thing to do, I thought, something any loving parent could do, and I gave it no further thought. I had experienced the true power of loving Oneness.

True Love

A heavy price is paid when we choose for separation from Source in that we deny ourselves access to Oneness. In that state of separation, we lose the ability to know and experience an integral aspect of our nature as creator beings—true Love. We say that we seek love, or we say we're "in love," but the love we are familiar with on the lower consciousness level is not the full experience of total and complete love that is available to us.

Because the ego is founded on the idea of separation and love is an experience of joining, it is easy to understand how only a certain amount of love can be experienced in the lower consciousness human condition. If there is fear that Oneness will wipe out our identities and rob us of our freedoms or our uniqueness, only a limited amount of love will be allowed. In the absence of love, separation is strengthened, thereby fuelling and maintaining fear, divisiveness, hierarchies, specialness, control, conflict, struggle and self-protection. We have forgotten that our uniqueness can never be taken away or in any way diminished, no more than a snowflake can lose its uniqueness.

The ego will attempt to convince you that love is transactional, that it can be withdrawn, measured out or withheld, or that it can be made to disappear. This is not the love that the higher Self knows. It is a substitute, or a small sampling of love, one that can be tolerated without threat to the separated ego. We all have the innate capacity to express love, yet in a state of separation, we choose it sparingly and at times cautiously. The truth is that love has never disappeared; it is the one thing that is eternal, unbreakable and unalterable. It is only the false self that can disappear from our experience, something that happens as we allow ourselves to experience more and more of that true love that is in our hearts.

True love is everything that the ego is not, and so true love will not sustain or support separation. When you feel drawn to loving someone, the ego might look for ways of distracting you, ways of convincing you that the love can't work, that it cannot last, that you are not worthy of it or that it is must be earned. In this way, love is seen as a threat to the ego because love is an act of joining, total acceptance and the absence of judgment. True love is not binding, nor is it coercive, restrictive, manipulative or transactional. True love can only be experienced when Oneness is allowed and accepted. Essentially, the ego cannot support and maintain true, complete expressions of love, for love is experienced in Oneness.

We've all had moments in which we were touched by love. Love catches us off guard—literally, when our barriers are down—and that is its essential nature. Love is forgiving, kind and intelligent. There is no ambivalence about it. Best of all, love does not need to be learned or developed, earned, negotiated, bartered or acquired. It is innate in each and every one of us. It is the essential nature of our Being. Love knows that everyone is deserving of love, which is why it is the one ingredient that is at the heart of the healing of humanity.

In accepting that we are a part of something far greater than our small individualities, we will, in fact, lose something, so our fears, at least at first, seem justified. If we are to accept love as the essence of our Being, we will be required to abandon much of what we believe to be true about ourselves because most of these beliefs are based on separation. When we know love, we open ourselves to Oneness, and so we lose the separate self, the one that believes it is possible to function independently from Source. Is that such a great price to pay for knowing true love?

As we let down the barriers and open the door to Oneness, it becomes easy to choose love in our interactions with others and with the world because love feels so good, it feels so right. The more you express love, the more will be available to be expressed, and its expression will become normal and natural. You will encounter many who have trouble loving themselves, but you will teach them to love themselves by your example. The love that you express will flow from you; it will have a direct impact on everything and everyone in your vicinity and beyond.

The choice for love is what will change the human condition; it is the greatest contribution that each one of us can make. Love unites in Oneness, the most powerful force in the universe. It can literally move mountains. The day we decide to join in Oneness, we will know that nothing can harm us. Oneness, or Love, is mankind's greatest and last and most important lesson. While the Aquarius climate does not sustain empty sentimentalism or excessive drama or emotionalism, it does know what love is because it feels so good.

Interestingly, the day I was working on this section was also the day my friend Helena had booked me as a witness for a wedding she was performing. While the couple had been together for thirty-four years, they had decided to make it official. As I was shown to the living room where the ceremony was to be held, I noticed the piles of CDs on a shelf, and on top of each pile was a different CD from the Rod Stewart jazz standards collection. Now that was a romantic occasion!

But this was not the usual wedding with fancy clothes and flowers and food. Quite the contrary. The bride-to-be had recently suffered serious medical problems, and they had rescheduled the wedding once already. She was weak and needed a walker to get around the house. She wore a simple but elegant white lace top with pants. Her husband remained by her side, never letting her out of his sight. It was a brief ceremony due to the bride's condition, and when Helena reached the vows of love and devotion, eyes began

CHAPTER 9 • AWAKENING TO ONENESS

to tear up. What was remarkable was the total, unwavering love they felt for each other. It was palpable and so very real. They were living true Oneness. They would celebrate their marriage in a more elaborate way once she felt better. Their love for each other had been officially declared, and that's all that mattered. What a beautiful gift to be a witness to this true Love and Unity.

The Healing of the Great Divide

I stand over here
You over there
When will we meet
And see eye to eye,
Heart to heart?

So many divisions
Black, white
Male, female
Straight, queer
Left, right

Where do we meet?
Do we have anything in common?
Yes,
Yes we do
We come from the same Source
An infinitely deep well of pure Love
Ever expanding,
Forever beaming its radiant Light
This Love is our common origin
And it is our common destiny

So don't forget
Go to the ground of Being
Where all roads meet
And I will see you there

Michael J. Miller

CHAPTER 10

The Creative Power of Mind

It is hard to recognize that thought and belief combine into a power surge that can literally move mountains. It appears at first glance that to believe such power about yourself is merely arrogant, but… (p)eople PREFER to believe that their thoughts cannot exert real control because they are literally AFRAID of them. (ACIM, Ch. 2, p. 38)

I Think, Therefore I'm Smart!

Over the past few years, my neighbour and I have enjoyed feeding the ducks on Roxboro Island near my condo. Out of the twenty or so that approached us for our daily handouts, one of them was bold enough to eat out of the palm of my hand. Every day he would make his way through the crowd, sometimes even jumping up and down in front of me until I reached down with a handful of treats.

It's a tiny island, more like a nature park, just off the larger island of Montreal, and the stream that runs between it and the main island is quite narrow. In the springtime, lush with the promise of fresh new vegetation, the island becomes an ideal spot for nesting. In a matter of weeks, mama ducks are leading their fuzzy little ducklings to water. Not long after, the little ones are following mama to their favourite feeding spot, where they begin to enjoy the corn and oatmeal we give them.

Late last winter, for some reason, the ducks stopped coming for their feedings. As the weeks passed, instead of the usual flooding caused by melting snow up river, the water levels dropped drastically, so that by the middle of May, the flow of fresh water around the island had completely stopped. By mid-June, the island was no longer an island. In light of this development, it then dawned on me that the ducks had most likely known better than to nest near receding waters.

How did they know this without the aid of weather alerts on their cell phones or news media? Everyone knows this was simply a natural function of innate survival instinct. Still, it's interesting to observe first-hand how they just knew it, without the need to think about it. They didn't have to vote on whether or not to move upstream or downstream, nor did they hold demonstrations in front of the mayor's office demanding freedom of choice. They didn't argue or debate the upcoming weather trends nor question the validity or accuracy of their basic, instinctual, internal messaging system. They didn't bother to check on their inventories to see if they had enough toilet paper or calculate how much money they could make by taking advantage of the impending low water levels. All together, they just got up and relocated. End of problem—which really was not a problem at all. It was just a situation that needed to be addressed, which they did, in a simple, uncomplicated, timely manner.

Humans are far more complex than ducks, and everyone—well, probably almost everyone—will say that we're smarter than our fine-feathered friends. Indeed, we have much more going for us than basic survival instinct. We can think for ourselves, analyze, investigate, question, debate, study and evaluate, think some more, then maybe take action or return to our thinking binges. Indeed, we have been given the wonderful gift of this thinking apparatus. Throughout the Era of Pisces, this skill has been greatly developed and enhanced, as can be seen by our tremendous achievements. However, while we have focused on developing this wonderful thinking instrument—a mutable trait of Pisces—we may have inadvertently done so at the expense of some of our other innate abilities, leaving us with a means of perception, learning and communication that is somewhat out of balance.

CHAPTER 10 • THE CREATIVE POWER OF MIND

The Source of Inspiration

As I was about to begin work on this chapter, I felt the urge to get back to some music lessons. One of my favourite piano teachers, Arthur Bird, had just posted a new course on how to read music using a simple approach he had developed. This was a great place to start, I thought. Having been busy with writing and consultations, I had barely touched that keyboard in months, and I was due for a refresher.

One of the lessons in this course presented a helpful visual aid for how to remember the notes by turning the staves ninety degrees to the keyboard. All of a sudden, I saw E-G-B-D-F on my keyboard. It was so simple! I sent Arthur a message thanking him for the new course and for the brilliant tip. His response was a perfect example of the subject I was preparing to write about. He replied, "Yeah, that idea to flip them around came to me just before nodding off to sleep one night, so I quickly wrote it down. I then wondered why it's not normally explained that way as it makes logical sense, doesn't it."

Everyone has had this experience. You're working hard to figure something out, trying to solve a problem, looking for a solution, and then nothing seems to work. You've given it your all, but you just can't see the light. Frustrated, or just plain tired, you give up, set it aside, and put your mind on something completely different. You go for a walk, mow the lawn, make plans for an evening out with your BFF, prepare supper or search online for that special item you want to buy. You just let it go. The next morning, just as you're about to get up and face a new day or, as in Arthur's case, as you are about to fall asleep, an idea just pops into your mind. Aha! That's it; that's your answer, your solution.

Sometimes an idea can come while sleeping, as was the case with Kekulé when he discovered the benzene ring. One night he had a dream of a serpent chasing its tail, from which he got the idea to connect the six carbon atoms in a circle. More often than not, the idea arises when you aren't even thinking about it, when you least expect it. When it comes, it seems so brilliant, so simple and, above all, so obvious. Why didn't I think of this before? Most of us are aware that our greatest ideas—our wonderful hunches—don't come from thinking alone. Actually, ideas do not come from thinking. So, where do inspired ideas or flashes of insight come from?

Looked at from the perspective of consciousness pioneers who are reaching up to a higher level of conscious awareness, the question takes on an entirely different meaning. To inspire, or in French, "inspirer," means to breathe in. It can also be seen as breathing in the Infinite Life Principle or God/Creator Source Energy. Sometimes, inspiration seems to come from "above" or beyond our usual thinking faculties, as though from a "higher mind." Our sense is that the idea came from somewhere "out there," somewhere else, or outside of us. This means that, whether or not we are fully aware of it, we already have the ability to connect to a source of intelligence or information that lies beyond the basic thinking level to a higher, inspired level.

This connection to a "higher mind" will begin to make sense and occur more frequently as we explore and experience the far-reaching possibilities of the fact that we are more than separate, independent body/mind beings residing in a 3-D material world. As direct expressions of Creator Source Energy, we naturally have inherited some of its attributes, for God, or Creator Source Energy, creates, or extends, as Itself. As it is said, "we were created in the image and likeness of God/Source." If we go back to Cause, before all manifestation, before form, before *us*, there is the Idea, and all inspired ideas emerge from that aspect of Source called Mind. As the original Idea emerges from the God/Creator Mind, it contains all the energy, light, intelligence, knowledge, inspiration and love needed for its full and right expression and manifestation. The original Idea is a whole, perfect and complete expression of Source Energy. Mind is a powerful intrinsic aspect of the Creative Life Principle, and as creator beings, we can—and do—tap into the power of Mind for our own creations.

A distinction needs to be made between Mind and our thinking apparatus. When we are aligned with the lower level of consciousness

… of the small self, the true, pure power of Mind cannot be wholly accessed nor used to its fullest capacity. The lower level of thinking comes from adherence to the belief in separation from Source, and so it is not fully inspired nor empowered. As we engaged in separation, we became independent thinkers, an activity that is highly valued in this age of abundant information. Thinking then rose above all other expressions. No longer fully connected to the Source of inspired ideas, we forgot that thinking is meant to serve Mind, and Mind is accessed through the higher consciousness of the true Self.

Some will point out that we have progressed much in the last few hundred years. Look at all we are capable of doing; look at everything we have accomplished, at everything we have created. We are much smarter, more intelligent, far more evolved than we were thousands of years ago. And, indeed, this is true, at least in part. If we look at what we have created, it is clear that even with our limited level of consciousness we have manifested some great accomplishments. However, the small self, or ego, can only access a limited portion of the energy of Mind. As its primary intention is to maintain separation from Source, when thinking is used in service of the ego, we are depriving ourselves of our full creator potential. Instead, we are limited to illusory expressions of fantasy and imagination, expressions that can never replace nor embody the full Reality of Creation.

The True Power of Mind

Another challenging aspect of what is being revealed today is that our minds have power—real power. It is through mind that we create our reality, the world in which we live and, consequently, the life we are experiencing. Our apparent experience of separation is a good example of the extent of the creative power of mind. No one, except for a few bold souls, would question the reality of this 3-D world. We have worked long and hard to build it, and we know it well, therefore it must be real. However, the full potential of Mind energy lies beyond the five physical senses, memory and beliefs, beyond that which is experienced in the lower consciousness state of the separated self.

The price paid for maintaining separation from Source is the absence of full creative power, while the price paid for regaining full power is giving up the idea of separation. This is one of the primary benefits of rising up, reconnecting with our true Self and reclaiming and reknowing our place in Oneness. Given how much we have already created on this planet in a state of limited consciousness, one can only imagine what we could manifest if we simply accessed our full creator potential.

As we release the lower consciousness mind and strengthen our connection with the higher Mind, we will become free of the limitations of our current 3-D body/mind experience. It will then be possible to explore beyond our old familiar boundaries in ways we have only imagined in fables and fiction. We will emerge beyond the limited ego sense of self into a vaster plane of experience. No longer bound, our experience will expand into infinity. The ego's domain, in fact, is extremely small, being limited to the five physical senses. There is so much more to be experienced than what the small self limits us to.

Some will say that they don't want more than what they have now because it's too overwhelming already. Who wants more; it's impossible to keep up with all the stuff that's coming out every day. Our lives have become exceedingly busy. Most of our waking hours are spent trying to figure things out, addressing issues and problems and mostly thinking. Some of these hours are spent processing distracting—and very often disturbing—information from media and entertainment. Not all of our thinking is creative, inspired, productive, helpful or even healthy. If it leads to fear, anxiety, depression or any other form of imbalanced or negative emotion, very likely the thinking was an expression of the lower state of consciousness of the ego. Thinking that follows inspired ideas leads to creative, joyful, uplifting, energizing, productive and helpful responses and action.

One day, I was feeling a little lost, perhaps a bit overwhelmed, as though I was caught between two very different levels of consciousness. I received the following bit of helpful insight from guidance: "Being in the higher level of consciousness, or awake, isn't just a matter of experiencing more of the same of what you are experiencing now, or what you perceive as competitive, dog-eat-dog world. When you move into the higher level of consciousness, you move into a place and experience of complete harmony where there is no competition because there is no lack, there is no need so it is a simple flow of Love and Life and energy and intelligence." Now that was uplifting!

To Think and to Know

As adept as we are at "using our minds," thinking can actually be an impediment to knowing, for knowing and thinking are not one and the same. In fact, thinking is not even needed for knowing. Ultimately, it is knowing that we seek, for in knowing, truth is experienced; whereas thinking alone is not always truthful. Ideas that emerge from Mind are already founded in true Knowing, since God/Source is whole, infinite, timeless and complete. An Idea is expressed from Mind as an opportunity for discovery and learning by those who will encounter it in manifestation. Knowing comes from the quiet place within, where it lies in waiting, where it has always been. Very often, knowing is the result of learning derived from direct first-hand experience, when the mind is free of thinking and thus open and ready to receive.

Everyone has had those experiences where you find yourself in a situation, or you look at something or someone and, without thinking, you just know what needs to be said or done. Maybe you saw an expression on your son's face as he walked in the door after an important exam, and you just knew what needed to be done. "Come in the kitchen. I just made your favourite cranberry chocolate chip cookies." This knowing came without forethought, simply from a feeling you had through observation, caring, compassion, inner wisdom and your natural connection with your son in Oneness.

The ego does not really want to know. It only thinks it knows and it will do whatever it takes to convince you that it knows. What it actually wants is to be right. The ego needs to be right in order to maintain its precious position as director of your lower state of consciousness and it does so in part by making a lot of noise through thinking. An added benefit of thinking for the small self is that while you are busy thinking, you are not listening or feeling, and thus are less likely to seek out and tap into the wisdom and inspiration of the true Self.

This thinking can take on many forms, such as logical deduction, ruminating over the past, analysis, investigation, memorization, comparison or measurement, or validation through data, science, reasoning and history. The more thinking you engage in, the stronger the ego's position. However, in order to move to a higher level of consciousness, you must be ready and willing to let go of what you think you know and make room for the unknown. This is not an easy point to process given that we have shifted into the age of boundless information, and also given that the keywords for Aquarius are "I know."

To truly know someone or something, we must be aligned with truth, and truth is only available in Oneness. In the separated state, we have thus far not fully known the true power of Mind. For the most part, we have only known thinking. Note how surprised you were when a brilliant idea came into your mind, whereas the opposite should be your experience, where you embrace the fact that brilliant ideas are normal and natural for beings that are connected with the higher Self, for beings that are expressions of the Infinite Life Principle. Once fully engaged in the higher level of consciousness, thinking then serves to develop, or even play with, the original, inspired idea. In this way, thinking is not an effortful, distracting, confusing or troubling activity. In fact, in service of Mind, thinking should be easy, enjoyable and fun.

Is there such a thing as coincidence? I'm starting to doubt it very much. I see signs all the time, and mostly they serve as support, confirmation and reinforcement in my daily activities; sometimes they are just humorous. Just before working on this section, I returned to a piano course I hadn't touched in quite a while: Eric

Satie's first *Gnossienne*. Interesting? This is a free time composition, without bars or signatures, named after a word he invented inspired by Gnosticism, a spirituality based on "knowing." The free flow of the beautiful melody exemplifies the free flow of knowledge when it is allowed to be expressed.

Because Minds Are Joined

Many studies on the power of mind and consciousness have emerged over the past several decades, covering a broad spectrum of perspectives from scientific to spiritual. Researchers have found common ground, resulting in a joining and sharing of studies and information in fields that, for several hundred years, have been held in a state of mutual exclusivity. It is particularly interesting to note those findings that are emerging as a result of collaborative efforts between science and spirituality. The fact that those working in these fields are dropping their boundaries and finding commonality is another indication that our collective consciousness is shifting from a world of divisiveness to one of inclusiveness, sharing, collaboration and community spirit. Consciousness, intelligence, the power of mind, energy, frequency and vibration are all subjects that are very much in tune with the climate of Aquarius, and more works in these fields are likely to be presented in the coming years.

This brings up another crucial bit of information that is at the heart of many new teachings: that our thoughts, individually and collectively, contribute to the experience of all beings on Earth at any given time. Recent studies have shown that our collective mindsets have a very real, tangible, measurable impact on the energy fields of humanity as well as on the planet. The way in which we experience our world is, therefore, the result of our combined thoughts and agreements, thoughts and agreements that we have freely chosen and expressed as beings that have access to creator power. This also sheds light on the fact that we are not "victims" of some discriminating, unfair, superior god force or some dark, controlling, manipulating secret societies or cabals. We are living the world we are collectively creating through the free use of our mind power. Since our thoughts and beliefs are the basis of our actions and decisions, as we think, so shall we create.

While we remain tethered to the lower 3-D level of consciousness, most of our perceptions and thoughts will be coloured by memories, conditioning, beliefs, habits, training, fear—the most powerful influencer—and the need of the ego to maintain its now increasingly precarious position. It is from this level of consciousness that we project our mind energies out into the world. We are effectively experiencing today the consequences of decisions and actions that began as thoughts that were projected sometime in the past. So it follows that what we will experience tomorrow will be the result of actions taken in response to—and in reaction to—thoughts we are holding today, hence the vital importance of paying attention to our mindset in each and every moment, since it is from our thoughts that the life experience of tomorrow is being brought forth.

What we need to be aware of is that tomorrow is being created now, and it will take on the flavour and colour of the thoughts we are cultivating now. When millions of people are enjoying a competitive sport with a vested interest in one team winning over the other, the me-versus-you, us-versus-them aspect of the human condition is reinforced. Competition, when taken seriously, is divisive in nature. Millions of people enjoying the thrill of an exciting, violent, good-versus-evil, dramatic television series, movie or game magnifies the propensity for conflict, adversity, opposition and claiming gains and wins for the small self, no matter the cost. In the same way, fear-inducing drama, media or entertainment reinforces fear in the human collective mindset.

What is being circulated in the form of dark conspiracies, nefarious plots, doom and gloom prophecies for the future of humanity, *has not yet been made manifest.* At this point, such information serves only to stir up and maintain fear, and to be in fear is to give away your power and sovereignty. Once you have given away your power, you can easily be manipulated and controlled by those desirous of such low consciousness behaviour. Since minds are joined,

CHAPTER 10 · THE CREATIVE POWER OF MIND

and together we create our tomorrow, to dwell on dark, terrifying thoughts is to contribute to their potential manifestation *sometime in the future*. Paying attention to our individual mindsets and making corrections as needed is what will ultimately lead to a more desirable future for humanity.

The idea that we are all connected on the level of mind may be difficult to comprehend at first. However, the implications are far-reaching. This means that with a revolutionary shift in consciousness, the world in which we live can shift completely to another level of existence, to another world, without necessarily having to work at it for centuries, without it taking thousands of years of evolution, without the necessity of wiping ourselves out and having to start over from scratch. The point is to choose the highest level of mind from which to function now so we can create the best possible tomorrow for all beings. Since we are all connected on the level of mind, every small adjustment we make in our own mind will contribute to the healing of the whole.

Your Thoughts Matter

At this time of transition between the old and the new, a period that holds tremendous potential for a shift in consciousness for humanity, it is important that we learn to pay attention to the activity of our thinking apparatus. When you look forward in time, do you see a dark, post-Orwellian world, or do you see a world inhabited by conscientious, compassionate beings that care as much for the planet as they do for each other? In the same way that you would not likely drink muddy water, you always remain free to choose what kind of data you will feed your thinking apparatus. Why not choose beautiful, uplifting, inspiring, kind, loving thoughts?

While some will recommend that you completely avoid the news, entertainment and social media, a moderate approach might be wiser. A minimum amount of information about current events may be useful and even necessary in order to perform your daily tasks. However, when you feel any sort of unbalanced emotion such as fear, anxiety, worry or concern, it is probably best to turn off the media and focus on a peaceful activity. You can always get another dose of news later.

As often as possible, take some time during the day to turn your attention to that quiet place within, where deep inner knowing is accessed. You will know that you have properly connected because it will feel good. After all, the true Self does not know fear, since what resides in Oneness can never be made less than perfect, whole and complete. While in that quiet place, ask for guidance, connect with those enlightened beings that are helping us during this time of transition. Listen, learn and let yourself be inspired as to how you can contribute by bringing the light into your daily activities. Sometimes a simple gesture or a kind word can have the greatest impact.

Pause once in a while and take note of the activity of the mind. Thinking will serve one of two masters: the separated self or the true Self. If there is an absence of peace, if there is overwhelming data being processed through the thinking apparatus, if there is an emotional charge behind the thoughts such as, for example, anxiety, fear, frustration or impatience, chances are that the thinking is being used in service of the small self. Amid all this noise, the voice of the true Self is not likely to be heard. In the absence of a connection with the higher Self, the ego thrives, and only the limited, lower state of consciousness can be accessed.

Once the state of mind has been identified, if needed, a simple correction can be made. Say "no thanks" to the ego's invitation, take a deep breath and turn your attention to the true Self. You remain always free to choose which voice you will listen to, although sometimes, you may need to say "no thanks" several times, and with firm conviction. The true Self has never left your side and remains always available to provide a perspective of truth, insight, wisdom and knowledge in any given situation. All that is needed is that you pause and remind yourself that you can make a different choice.

CHAPTER 10 · THE CREATIVE POWER OF MIND

Heart and Mind

We have learned to value thinking more than we have learned to value feeling. When we are experiencing feelings, we are perceived as being in a lower level of experience. But more than that, no distinction is made between wonderful feelings such as love, caring and joy, and ego-based emotions such as fear, hatred or anger. This is unfortunate because feeling is one of the most effective ways of gaining insight into what is occurring in any given situation. Thinking, by its very nature, automatically erects a barrier to feelings, while feelings can indicate which level of mind we are aligned with.

What we are missing when we value thinking over feeling is that emotions may inform us that something is wrong or out of balance when there is, for example, discomfort, fear, anxiety, unhappiness or distress of any kind. You can then acknowledge that you made a wrong turn, or you made a poor choice, no doubt based on an invitation from the ego. Or perhaps you acted on a desire that was not inspired from the true Self. Feelings can then be used to get a sense of the best course of action to take if a correction is needed. The right course will feel good. When a truly inspired idea has been received, the good feeling it brings up is undeniable. As an added bonus, having consciously reconnected with Mind, you will feel supported as you follow through with the appropriate actions. In this way, thinking, understanding, observation and feeling can all be used in a balanced, helpful way.

Try thinking like a child, free of the past, without expectations, beliefs or conditioning. Simply be open to inspiration, and watch as the best thoughts emerge, unhindered by overthinking, analysis or shoulds and shouldn'ts. Breathe deeply and pay attention to the feeling. When mowing the lawn or washing the car or preparing your family meal, feel the appreciation and gratitude for the tools, the abundance, for whatever is available to you in the moment. When going out for a walk in the park or in nature, join with the trees and the birds and the breeze; feel the beauty of Life flowing around and through you. Let whatever you are involved with, whatever you are doing, teach you. Embrace the knowing being made available in every moment through feeling, welcoming, openness, curiosity and quiet observation.

When feeling joy and peace, most likely you have been functioning in alignment with your higher Self. It may not be as gratifying as the feeling you get after overcoming some major dramatic challenge, but that kind of gratification belongs to the ego. Whenever you recognize that you have been functioning from the higher Self, taking a moment to acknowledge this healthy experience will help strengthen your resolve to repeat it more frequently. Celebrate it. To add a little icing on that cake, give yourself a hug and feel some love for yourself. A sprinkling of self-love makes this journey truly wonderful, inspiring and joyful.

Mind in Motion

The expression of Mind being new every moment means that anything and everything can shift, change, heal, grow and evolve when we are connected to the higher Self. At each moment we stand at the threshold of unlimited possibilities, with access to our own best knowing and inspiration. As we begin to remember our place in Oneness and start to tap into the true power of Mind, we can expect healing of ourselves, of the human collective and of the planet. In this way, we will be rising above the level of any problem which was caused by decisions made in the lower state of consciousness, to where the true solution can be found—in Mind.

We believe that matter is powerful and that one thing can destroy another. But Mind is far more powerful than matter since Mind is infinite and it cannot be destroyed. In fact, by putting our attention on body/form/matter, we diminish our experience tremendously. We exclude the greater potential of who and what we are as expressions of Mind, connected to infinite energy, wisdom, love and light. We are living only a tiny bit of reality, which we mistake for the full experience of life.

CHAPTER 10 • THE CREATIVE POWER OF MIND

While walking to the store one day, as I often do, I reminded myself that I am Mind, and it is Mind that is moving me as I am walking. Maybe it appears as though muscles and joints and various body parts are doing the work, but it is Mind that is creating the movement. The body only serves to identify me on this lower level of perception. If Mind is the Source of all expression, then it must be that *I am being from Mind now*. I knew what these words meant, I had understood and appreciated them intellectually, but this time was different.

All of a sudden, the words "I am being from Mind now" took on a sense of immediacy, a sense of electrifying, palpable accessibility. They weren't just nice words—albeit really nice words. I saw that we don't experience things on the material physical level alone, since all is experienced in Mind. The idea of being from Mind now ignited a great curiosity for an experience of what lies beyond the physical, sensory level. I could teleport my way to the store if I wanted to. We are, in fact, always teleporting ourselves from one place to the other, since all of our impulses come from our mind. By the same token, this means that you are reading this book as Mind, only believing you are reading it as a separate thinking self, sitting in a chair, perhaps wearing reading glasses.

What appears as matter, what appears as physical, is not set in stone, nor is it unchangeable. It only appears as matter, as form, as body from the lower state of consciousness we currently adhere to. The essence of all Life, all manifestation, including what appears as matter is actually an Idea expressed from Mind that unfolds as energy, spirit, love and light. It is because of our choice to experience things from the limited 3-D level that gives matter its dense, solid form. The essence of Life is not solid, so anything that appears as solid can be experienced in other dimensions of expression. To be aware of the movement of Life at the level of body alone is to be aware of only a small portion of the movement of Life.

This means that by connecting with the full energy and power of Mind, we are no longer bound by the limitations of the 3-D experience and can manifest our desires without the need to rely on lower consciousness means. Once we are fully aware that idea comes before form, form can then be made to shift simply by changing the idea. By changing how we see the body, we can experience the correction of a physical defect or even the healing of a serious illness. Imagine communicating with each other without the need of handheld devices simply through telepathy, where minds are joined. Imagine travelling around the globe without the need of vehicles, simply by teleportation, as a result of the desire to be in another place. Or perhaps you may want to manifest a loaf of bread, gluten-free, and there it is, in your hand.

As we release the boundaries and limitations that are based on beliefs and conditioning, our future potential becomes truly unlimited. To carry this line of thought is more significant than we could possibly imagine, since our thoughts are an integral aspect of our experience, and they will be crucial to the shift in consciousness for the entire human collective.

What we need to ponder and bring to mind as frequently as possible is that what emanates from Mind has perfect order, beauty and harmony. If Mind is in all things, then encased in this physical form we call the body, we will find Mind, eternal Life, wholeness and perfection. From Source, the breath of Life is expressed, and so Life flows through every inch, every molecule and every cell of our Being. I am, We are and have always been expressions of Mind. As we heal the inner and outer divisiveness that distracts us from this truth of who and what we are, we will come together and know ourselves as One in Mind.

There is a place to go in the mind that is quiet, rich and full of possibilities. That place is not the same one that is usually engaged in the busyness of the world or in thinking. This is a different aspect of mind, and it seems to open up to infinite possibilities, as though the universe is opening up before me. As my guide points out: "That's the level of mind, the place of mind that needs to be accessed more and more frequently until it is the only place of mind from which you come no matter what is going on in the world. It is a place of mind that is not limited by physical or sensory data or

CHAPTER 10 · THE CREATIVE POWER OF MIND

input. And it is accessible at all times no matter how much sensory data appears to be coming at you."

Exercise: If I Ruled the World

A few years ago, I discovered a most beautiful song written by Cyril Ornadel and Leslie Bricusse: "If I Ruled the World." The version I first heard, and the one I still prefer, was performed by Tony Bennett. The first time I heard the song, I couldn't hold back the tears. It was so touching and heart-warming and expressed what I felt humanity needed. Look it up on YouTube and see if it might inspire you to do this exercise. If you are a bit of an empath, you may want to grab a tissue. After listening to the song, grab a pencil and paper or your tablet or whatever device you like to use for jotting down notes. Ask yourself if you ruled the world, what kind of world would we live in? What would you like to see for every man and woman? For every child? For planet Earth and all its life forms?

> Child of God, you were created to create the good, the beautiful, and the holy. Do not lose sight of this. (ACIM, Ch. 1, p. 19)

Prayer: I See a World

I see a world where death is no more.
I see a world where hospitals are turned into condos
because no one is sick.
I see a world where war is unthinkable
and love and brotherhood reign supreme.
I see a world where joy is everywhere and fear is gone.
I see a world of total peace and freedom and safety.
I see a world where all suffering ceases to exist.
I see Heaven on Earth.
I see eternity.
I see being able to finally relax.
No reason to be defensive.
Loss and separation don't exist.
We are all One.
All is well forevermore.
Amen.

Michael J. Miller

CHAPTER 11

Higher Ground

You have no idea of the tremendous release and deep peace that comes from meeting yourselves and your brothers totally without judgement. When you recognize what you and your brothers ARE, you will realize that judging them in ANY way is without meaning. (ACIM, Ch. 3, p. 60)

Yeah, but What about Them?

While the idea of a united humankind working together in harmony for the good of all may sound very attractive, it may seem more like an unrealistic dream—or at least not likely to be made manifest any time soon. You look around, maybe recall the news you watched the night before or an argument you had with a coworker, then you shake your head. There is no way that you could—or even would want to—experience Oneness, let alone acknowledge being of "one mind" with that "insert what you think of him/her here." You have nothing in common with them, never will, and, as far as you can tell, you couldn't possibly belong to the same Oneness. Come to think of it, maybe you aren't even from the same galaxy. If that's what Oneness means, at least until things change, I think I'd prefer to remain in a state of separation, thank you very much. Surely, there are better people out there to be "One" with—a conclusion that was very likely arrived at through the use of the thinking apparatus alone, without checking in with the higher Self.

While you remain always free to choose how you will see, you may want to rethink that point of view. To judge another is to assign attributes based on conditioning, culture, education, memory, tradition, views, beliefs, norms and standards acquired while in the separated state. In other words, to judge another is to view them through the tainted lens of lower consciousness programming of the ego; it is to attribute meaning outside of Oneness, devoid of the love and clear sight of the true Self. Since minds have power, thoughts of judgment support and maintain the situation as it is perceived. To judge another implies that you know them in the depths of their Being, while you do not even know who and what *you* truly are. The more significant and, at the same time, more helpful question would be, why do we judge others in the first place?

In the dualistic state of separation, the normal and almost unavoidable course of action will most often be motivated by the deeply rooted need of the small self, or ego, to protect itself and preserve its separateness. In Oneness, the ego has no place, and a very easy and not terribly creative or imaginative way of sustaining separation is through judgment. To find something to judge or criticize in another serves to establish a boundary, strengthening "me" and "them," ensuring the preservation of separateness. By pointing out errors, defects or faults, the other is rejected, diminished and rendered unworthy.

A distinction must be made between judgment and discernment. It's one thing to judge with the intent to belittle, find fault, condemn, create distance or put up barriers. It's another thing to observe the facts of a situation in order to know how to respond in the most appropriate, kind, loving, respectful, uplifting and helpful way. While we function in the lower consciousness state, understandably, many errors will be found, providing much fodder for the ego's game of judgment. However, as we ascend to our true Self and join with the higher Mind, what appear as errors will always be recognized as opportunities for learning and for removing the barriers to knowing who and what we are in truth.

CHAPTER 11 • HIGHER GROUND

The Hidden Side of Judgment

Why would someone look at another, point the finger, criticize, condemn, find fault and diminish their worth through judgment? An old saying sheds some light on this question: Some people cut off the heads of others to make themselves taller. This makes sense in a lower consciousness state where self-worth and self-love are not taught or encouraged, let alone truly experienced. How can you love and value yourself when you have forgotten all about your true Self and are only aware of a tiny aspect of who and what you are—a small, made-up, bumbling, separated self residing in an imperfect physical form destined to wither and die. Lacking in self-worth, the quick and easy way to gain a semblance of worth, even if it's only a tiny crumb, is to reduce it in others. It's easier to point the finger outside than it is to remove the hidden inner garbage, claim your worth as an expression of the Infinite Life Principle/God and love yourself for no reason other than to love is the natural expression of life.

Since judgment serves to maintain the illusion of separation, it is contrary to Oneness and will delay the experience of the higher state of consciousness we claim to desire. Judgment came into our experience when Oneness was rejected, and love was withheld. When we exclude another through any form of judgment, we are denying ourselves the opportunity to reach beyond the limited state of separation and know and experience who we truly are as loving, inclusive creator beings. In this limited state, we cannot make those significant contributions that will lead to the healing of humanity. If we can't recognize the wholeness, the good, the divinity or the perfection in another, we will not be able to recognize it in ourselves either. That's a heavy price to pay for maintaining a state of smallness.

It is said that how you see another is a reflection of how you see yourself, or what you believe to be true about another is what you believe to be true about yourself. If we see something in another, it is most likely because we already know it, and what we know is usually the result of personal experience. Since we are creator beings, ultimately, our beliefs and thinking patterns are reflected in the reality we are creating; they are the source cause of our experience. However, no one wants to admit to—let alone assume responsibility for—their own less-than-glorious behaviour or character traits. To get rid of this unpleasant burden, we project what we don't want to see about ourselves onto others instead.

Taking Out the Trash

This radical line of thought may jar you into sudden revelations about those limiting beliefs and thinking patterns that define who and what you are. However, to acknowledge these patterns and explore their meaning in the context of your unique life journey can provide tremendous learning opportunities and ultimately great relief. Having been sent to stand in the corner by my first-grade teacher because I used a French word while answering a question in an English school no doubt seeded the fear of being judged if I dared express myself. Then, of course, there was the matter of having been raised Catholic with the stain of sin on my soul from the moment I was born, and my lack of worthiness for having been born in a female body, since women are worth less than men, and my inability to fit in given my interest in strange spiritual subjects, and my lack of socially accepted academic credentials, and the list goes on and on and on.

Fortunately, all of our life situations can be turned into extraordinary learning opportunities when we realize that they reflect what we believe to be true about ourselves. This is the moment at which we can abandon victimhood and reclaim our power. When I realized that I had chosen these circumstances for my own healing, another huge pile of garbage went out. My fear of being judged or punished, or alienated was a reflection of a deeply rooted belief in my unworthiness. I was my own worst judge and critic, and I expected this from the world outside of me. I had brought these situations into my life so that I could eventually feel the pressure of these mistaken beliefs and ultimately decide that this was not what

CHAPTER 11 · HIGHER GROUND

I wanted, this was not who I am; I wanted to experience the truth of who and what I am.

Once I realized this, I felt so much gratitude for my life journey, for all of its ups and downs and challenges. Any lingering or deeply buried sadness or disappointment I may have harboured began to fade. This was an incredible revelation, for it now allowed me to acknowledge my worth. The experience of my divine wholeness was at hand for the simple reason that it was my birthright as a Source Energy Being. No other justification was needed. All that was needed was to consciously make the choice to see myself in a new way. All events, interactions and situations could then be seen as neutral, no longer tainted by past experience, conditions, fear, beliefs or programming. Any situation or any encounter with another could then be embraced without the burden of judgment, with the simple, untainted, childlike curiosity to know its true meaning as an expression of Source energy.

As we move forward on this journey of reclaiming the truth of who we are, plenty of garbage will rise to the surface, mostly the garbage that stands in the way of the experience of our true Self. And, well, we know what to do with garbage. Fortunately, we don't need to spend a whole lot of time sifting through it. All that is needed is that we recognize it for what it is, an ego construct, therefore nothing but a lie. Besides, are we not the ones who have chosen our experiences? Ouch. That's not something we want to deal with, right? Nonetheless, it is the one thing that will allow us to reclaim our power. And so it is that we can now be grateful for our learning opportunities.

The early lessons of *A Course in Miracles* now made complete sense. We really don't know what anything means until we release the confidence in what we think we know. That's one of the toughest lessons for a Moon in Aquarius native. However, the wonderful upside is that being from a place of not knowing clears the way for the greatest potential for discovery and for experiencing something new. Now that sounds great for this Moon in Aquarius native.

> Beloved one, nothing that you have ever done or chosen to do has been wrong or a mistake, sinful. Never. It has been a free choice for the experience of it, and you are wealthy in that experience. (Jeshua Online—Daily Message)

Embracing the Backstory

If we are going to proceed with our desire to create a new world, we will need to reclaim our true power as creator beings. Since our thoughts matter, a good place to start is to learn to look and see in a new way. Every time we look at someone or something we have the freedom to choose how we will see them. How we see determines our experience of that person or thing. How we feel should also be taken into consideration, as it provides valuable information on our level of consciousness. Whenever there is fear or discomfort or lack of peace, it is a clear indicator that we are not centred and therefore not aligned with the higher Self. In this way, by paying attention to our reactions and responses as we interact with others and go about our daily activities, we come to learn much about ourselves, and so all of our interactions, all of our experiences, become invaluable learning opportunities.

Although the idea of reincarnation is not recognized in all traditions or cultures, as consciousness expands, there may be increasing awareness of past lives. This will also extend to parallel and even future lives since time is an aspect of the limited 3-D body/mind level of consciousness. Once we become aware of the fact that we have lived many lives and have experienced much in our countless journeys, it may be easier to release judgment of ourselves and of others. Chances are, we've done it all, and so who are we to judge another. While it is not necessary to dig up the past or analyze every detail of our histories, on occasion, helpful snippets might come to mind.

For example, you may get a sudden flash that explains why you are so fearful of long car rides. In a past life, you lost control while you were driving, and the car veered off into a ditch. In that tragic accident, you lost a family member. Okay, that makes sense now. Or

CHAPTER 11 · HIGHER GROUND

perhaps you recall a moment when you were a soldier during the First World War, and once on the field, you just couldn't pull the trigger and kill another human being. Caught between honouring God's commandments and those of your military commander, you felt trapped and confused. You walked off the field and have carried the shame and guilt ever since. This may explain why you can't hold down a job in this lifetime. Damned if you do, damned if you don't. Even with just a semblance of a backstory, it can be easier to release whatever issue you may be struggling with. You remind yourself of your true divine origin, you love yourself for your choices and your efforts regardless of their level of enlightenment, you learn whatever lesson is presented and you let it go. God/Source Energy does not, nor will it, express judgment, for it is founded in Love.

This applies to your perceptions of others as well. As you begin to consider the possibility that there is more to you than the 3-D body/mind aspect, that there is a higher Self within you, the same will need to be considered when you look at another person. No matter who they are, no matter what they seem to have done, no matter how low their current state of consciousness appears from your perspective, they too have a higher Self within them, and they too are expressions of the Creative Life Principle/God. Your function as a participant in the healing of humanity is to rise above the shared lower state of consciousness so that you can fully appreciate the truth of that other one.

We love our stories; just look at the popularity of our film and television industries. We also like to know the reason for just about everything. Why did he do this; why did she do that? Armed with this very limited information as to why a situation is as it is, we then choose how we will see it. However, rather than judging or criticizing another for behaviour that does not meet with your approval—approval that is based on scanty knowledge at best—imagine what they might have experienced in the past, or perhaps even in a past life, something that might have profoundly affected the behaviour and beliefs they now carry. Everyone has a backstory, and we all have plenty of imagination. If it can relieve you of the need to justify another's behaviour through judgment or criticism, if it can help you rise above your limited, ego-based perspective, try imagining what their backstory might have been.

Maybe your cousin's obsession with money is a result of a past life spent in extreme poverty after having been robbed of everything he owned. He spent the remaining years of that life on the streets, begging for food. Perhaps an old high school friend has no desire for worldly accomplishments, having worked himself to the bone in a previous life. Maybe your work colleague suffered a paralyzing illness in a past life and is now intent on enjoying the body by spending all of her free time in fitness and sports activities.

Make up any story that might fit your current picture of that one so the door may open to seeing them in a new way. It does not matter whether or not this is the truth of the person's story. What matters is that you accept that they have a backstory, and they have chosen their life for its unique learning opportunities, even the most challenging, just as you have. This point alone should help you know them through feeling rather than the limitations of thinking. What matters is that you have nothing on which to base your judgments, criticism or condemnation. What matters is that you want to be the presence of love, and that requires letting go of judgment and rising to your higher level of consciousness. In fact, it requires letting go of everything you think you know about that one so you can be free to see what they truly are as expressions of Source Energy/God.

The practice of forgiveness is a significant aspect of our healing journey as it releases many of the blockages and burdens that prevent us from moving forward. Forgiveness does not require that you spend your life uncovering all your hidden thoughts and memories. That would be an impossible task because the ego can churn out as many lies and distortions as you can forgive—and then some, and probably ten times faster. Forgiveness requires the abandoning of judgment, first and foremost, which means abandoning judging yourself and your perceived mistakes. By abandoning judgment of yourself, you will effectively be forgiving yourself. In so doing,

CHAPTER 11 · HIGHER GROUND

you will be in a better position to love yourself. By engaging in this process, it will be easier to forgive and love others.

While we are not responsible for another person's choices, we are responsible for how we see others. We have the choice to look with the eyes of Love and Unity from our higher consciousness Self, or we can look from the limited, divisive perspective of the ego, with judgment. If we see someone messing up and that's all we see, we are validating, sustaining and strengthening that position for ourselves and for that one. Through our vision, thoughts and beliefs, we are maintaining separation and divisiveness in the world we are creating. If we are not willing to accept and see that there is a divine one in the person before us, not only are we limiting our experience, but we will not be willing to accept that there is a divine one in us.

If we see that same someone who is messing up also as a divine one who could behave differently but who is temporarily choosing to behave in a less than divine manner, since we are of one Mind, we provide that one with the opportunity to see differently. We are thus breaking an agreement we made with that one to see them as less than whole. We are saying, no, I'm not going to see you that way anymore. I want to experience you in a different way. Instead, I choose to see the wholeness of you, that one that is the expression of God/Source. As we choose to see differently, we provide the other with an opportunity to see themselves differently. Nothing needs to be said or written or shared on any social media device since this is done on the level of Mind, through the shift in vibration and energy of our thoughts where we are joined with our true Self, where true power resides. By shifting the way in which we see another, we begin to explore what Oneness means, and the healing of all begins.

When it comes to guilt, it's a game you will never win. Everyone has some kind of guilt tucked away in their house of garbage—everyone! To feel guilty for our less-than-perfect and, at times, even shameful creations is easy. Having experienced hundreds of lifetimes throughout the Age of Pisces, where guilt can be laid on thicker than cold molasses, everyone is familiar with that feeling. However, guilt won't get us anywhere, and it serves no purpose, at least not a valid purpose. This game of sin, guilt, fear and punishment has been played for thousands of years, and it's getting old. Yet, it is still entirely without foundation. How can there be a belief in a loving God/Source along with a belief in judgment, condemnation and punishment? Clearly, this line of thought has been developed by beings in a lower state of consciousness. A loving parent would simply correct a misguided child and not condemn them to eternal hell and damnation. Instead, they would embrace them with a big loving hug.

While wholeness cannot be destroyed, it can only be ignored or forgotten. Each person therefore always has access to their wholeness, to their original divine expression. This is why there are times when the seemingly least holy individuals will express surprising, even unexpected, clarity of vision, insight, intelligence or wisdom. Somehow that wholeness or that divinity manages to seep through past the ignorance and become expressed.

We must remember that, together, with each of our unique qualities and journeys, we are members of one family, the family of humanity. There are infinite possibilities and expressions in creation, and that is what makes creation so exquisitely beautiful. In Unity there is acceptance, support and a natural appreciation for the other, for our differences and for our uniqueness. It is the subtle differences and the variations expressed by each member that make humanity beautiful, inspiring and powerful. We must now become aware of the fact that all parts belong to the Whole so we can know, without limitation, the magnificence of Life in Movement.

Exercise: Releasing the Error

Look back at a recent or past event that left you feeling less than deserving, something you said or did that left you feeling guilty or ashamed, perhaps angry with yourself, something you regretted, something you still feel bad about. I shouldn't have said that. I'm such an idiot; how could anyone love me. I can't possibly love myself. I keep screwing up. I wasn't kind, I was impatient and judgmental. I was jealous of my neighbour. I shouldn't have gotten angry with my boss.

Knowing that you did your best given your state of consciousness at the time, recognizing this as an opportunity to learn, an opportunity to grow and to raise your level of consciousness, you can now simply let it all go and give yourself a nice big hug. Be grateful for the learning opportunity that *you have brought into your experience*. Assuming responsibility for our experiences makes it easier to accept, learn and let go. Breathe deeply and hug yourself again. Now, the hard part: *feel the love*. By feeling the love for yourself, you are becoming reacquainted with your true Self, and you are reknowing your true worthiness as an expression of Source Energy/God. In this way, you will be able to acknowledge the worth of others.

Take the Lead

Some will say: Well, they are choosing and creating their own reality, their poverty or their misery. We're told that we are not responsible for another person, and so it's up to them to assume responsibility for themselves. And up to a certain point that would be accurate. However, we are responsible for how we see, and that way of seeing would not be compassionate. It would be a cold perspective, hence a low-level Aquarius way of seeing, and so not the ultimate experience for the consciousness pioneer, healer or light worker. What if their purpose here is to provide *you* with an opportunity to be compassionate?

While out for a walk with a neighbour one day, we passed by a man who appeared to be homeless. I say "appeared" because this is not what we typically see in the neighbourhood. He was squatting on a large duffle bag, leaning up against the brick wall of the bank. I tried to catch his eye to see if he needed anything, but he was busying himself with something in a bag on his lap. I asked my neighbour if he had seen this man before. He replied that he had not and then added, "but he chose to live like this."

Well, yes, maybe, but... There is something fundamentally wrong with what is becoming a common response these days. "You have the world you are creating," some cold-hearted New Agers will say. Yes, it is true; each one has what he or she has chosen. To apply this principle to oneself can be very helpful if you know what to do with it. Yes, I have chosen to be an idiot today or this year or throughout my life, but now I would like to change that. To accept responsibility for our choices is the first step toward healing and, ultimately, experiencing a higher level of consciousness. But, what is our function relative to another when they are responsible for their own life choices?

To look at another and judge them for their choice by saying "they chose it" is to miss the mark. Because someone chooses to believe that they are inherently worthless, or anything less than deserving of respect, dignity, wholeness and perfection, does not mean that we must or even should agree with them. To agree with them and not see the truth of who they are as expressions of Source Energy is to nurture and support their illusory sense of imperfection. To limit ourselves to this way of seeing is to turn down an opportunity to be the presence of love—the one thing the world needs most at this time.

The wonderful movie *Take the Lead* conveys a powerful message about the importance of the way in which we choose to see each other. It tells the story of how ballroom dance instructor Pierre Dulaine, so elegantly played by Antonio Banderas, introduced dance to a group of teens in a New York City high school detention class. The core message is that everyone deserves respect: for oneself and for others. No matter how self-deprecating these young men and women were, he refused to accept their views of themselves. Instead, he treated them with utmost respect and dignity, as though they were royalty and not the down-on-their-luck losers from a rough part of town they so energetically portrayed. His unwavering dedication to this way of seeing resulted in life-changing breakthroughs for this wonderful group of youth.

When you cross paths with others throughout the day, instead of buying into what they are projecting about themselves, why not take the lead, open your heart, set aside your limited vision and be curious to see who is truly there. That is the meaning of the miracle as taught in *A Course in Miracles*: a shift of perception, another way of looking and seeing. Look for the soul, the light, the beauty that lies hidden behind that other one's distorted view of himself or herself. You will then be in the world in a new way, as a true consciousness pioneer or teacher of God, in a way that will contribute to the healing of humanity.

Breaking the Agreement

The following is a simple exercise from *The Healing of Humanity* for facilitating the healing of a relationship that has become entangled in the false definitions of the ego. Keeping in mind that special relationships are sustained by mutual agreements, to withdraw our agreement is to break the bonds of the special relationship. The relationship now becomes an opportunity for healing and becomes what the Course refers to as a holy relationship. There is only one condition for the success of this exercise, without which it will not work: One must be fully ready to release the agreement. This means no longer seeing the other through the filters of memory, beliefs, definitions and judgments. This means releasing whatever benefits one derives from the relationship, whether positive or negative. It means being ready to be in a new way with this person.

Find a quiet place to sit and meditate for a few minutes. This is an exercise that you will be practising on your own, in the absence of the other person. Since minds are joined, there is no need for the other person to be present for this exercise to be effective. In fact, to have the other present might distract you from the full clarity available when you are in the quiet centre of your mind. This exercise will, however, be facilitated in partnership with guidance, so it is most appropriate to invite your guide to join you.

Once peace has been established, imagine yourself going back in time, before you were born, or simply outside the dimension of time, to that moment where your souls made the initial agreement to journey together for a 3-D body/mind experience. In this peaceful frame of mind, outside the confines of roles, definitions and memories of life in the state of separation, invite the other to join you. Imagine that you are pure spirit, soul or mind and that the other who has now joined you is also pure spirit, soul or mind.

You may begin by thanking the other for joining you in this exercise. Next, in your own words, clearly state your intention regarding the healing of the relationship. For example, you may let him or her know that you no longer wish to maintain an ego-based agreement. Thank them for having played along with you in your imaginary game of separation and for having provided you with an opportunity for learning. Let the other know that you are now releasing them from the agreement that binds you in the dream state and keeps the both of you from experiencing your divine wholeness. Without the false definitions and biases of your ego, what remains is the divine Self that God/Creator is being in your brother or sister. You may feel great relief and joy as false definitions are being released. With the blocks to the presence of love removed, true joining or communion can occur.

This is not an exercise that needs to be repeated; however, if you were not completely ready to release the agreement when you first did the exercise, it might be helpful to repeat it, as needed. All that is needed now is that you practise being with this person in a new way. If you were truly ready to see this special relationship transformed into a healed, holy relationship, you are likely to see evidence of this healing. While there is no need to tell the other person that you performed this exercise because it is never about the other person, you may be pleasantly surprised when he or she responds to you in a new way. You will then have first-hand evidence that minds are joined and that every little miracle, every little shift in perception can contribute to the healing of humanity. This is the power of mind being used in a new, uplifting way.

CHAPTER 11 · HIGHER GROUND

Forgive Me

Judgment hurts
Yet it's so cherished
I think sometimes there's something wrong with me
Why did I do the things I did?
Why do I get these negative thoughts and images?

But then I remember that I deserve and need to be loved
And I look at things in a different light,
With more compassion for myself and others.

Maybe something difficult happened to them
And that's why they act the way they do;
I, too, am doing the best I can
With what I know at each moment.

Would it really hurt to let in a little love,
For myself and for others;
Just open my heart,
And forgive?

Michael J. Miller

CHAPTER 12

A New Beginning

We only start again an ancient journey long ago begun that but seems new. We have begun again upon a road we travelled on before and lost our way a little while. And now we try again. Our new beginning has the certainty the journey lacked till now. (ACIM, Manual, p. 75)

Stop!

Life on planet Earth in the body/mind dimension has certainly provided wonderful learning opportunities for those who have chosen this experience. Given everything we have learned, we're ready to make some changes, and especially experience more of who and what we are. An interesting aspect of this brief study of the Eras is that it brings to light the backward precession of the equinoxes through the twelve signs of the zodiac. If, as we are now learning, we are responsible for the creation of our reality, it makes one wonder why we created a planetary system with a rather unusual trajectory. Given the discomfort that this backward motion would eventually cause, it was inevitable that one day, we would cry Stop! Was this a design flaw? Why would such a feature be incorporated if it was bound to cause problems? Perhaps we should ask the engineers. Oh, that's us!

It appears that, while exercising our freedom to create a world according to our own design, an aspect of us—probably the higher Self—made sure that one day we would be required to pause and reflect on our creations. This backward, ever-tightening mechanism was very likely built into our creation for that very purpose.

Perhaps we should be grateful for having included this triggering device in our creation, as it ensured that one day we would stop and reconsider what it is that we want to experience. Perhaps we should be grateful for the aspect of us, no matter how small, that reached out and asked that the truth of who and what we are be revealed. Maybe we should feel some love for ourselves, for it was in making the call that so much is now being brought forth. As we begin to reknow ourselves, our transformation from low-consciousness to high-consciousness beings has begun, and this we should celebrate.

Lessons from the Past

The transition into the Era of Pisces 2000 years ago presented tremendous learning opportunities for the human collective. Given the unique characteristics of the Pisces climate, this transition may have held the greatest potential for change, for facilitating, first and foremost, the healing of the idea of separation from Source. At its highest level of vibration, Pisces is the ideal climate for embracing the infinite flow of Life and for nurturing the experience of unity consciousness, love, light, wholeness and abundance for all, while honouring every facet of its expression.

These higher consciousness attributes were at the heart of the wonderful teachings brought to us by Jeshua/Jesus, where we learned that we could rise from an ego-based, small self, limited awareness to a much higher level as expressions of God/Creator Source Energy. We were invited to release ancient limiting beliefs and claim our true worth as infinite, creator beings, not limited by the lower body/mind consciousness. The ultimate lesson of Pisces was unconditional Love and the bringing together of the human collective, that which would once and for all heal all forms of division and separation. This lesson would have been very much welcomed as a foundation stone for the climate of Aquarius, as it touches on its humanitarian, community-oriented nature.

Looking back now, it appears that the gap between Aries and Pisces may have been a bit too wide to bridge, given the limited consciousness held by the human collective at the time. The lower level survivalist, materialistic, fear-based, divisive, self-serving, competitive mindset acquired over the previous Eras had become so deeply entrenched in the human condition that it was next to impossible to consider, let alone embrace, the more subtle, divine attributes inherent in the climate of Pisces. As such, we were not quite ready to accept the truth of our wholeness, our divine origins as Sons and Daughters of a loving Creator, Father/Mother God.

As a result, the unlimited, expansive potential of the Era of Pisces was then experienced from the low level of consciousness held at the time. So it is that, for the past 2000 years, we have experienced heightened drama, belief systems and teachings based on sin, guilt, fear, lies, control, fantasy, divisiveness and an almost complete denial of the Oneness of Life. The one point we mostly agree on is that it is possible to experience separation from Source, and now we are learning that this is not even possible, that it is an illusory experience of our own making.

Fortunately, the gap between Pisces and Aquarius is not as great as that between Aries and Pisces, and so it may be easier to bridge. Also, it is only one step down the ladder, rather than a leap from the bottom of one ladder to the top of another, as was the case during the transition from Aries to Pisces. Given the great discomfort and struggle experienced by countless souls on Earth at this time, the teachings being brought to us in answer to our calls for help may be easier to embrace. We want something better. What we have been experiencing is no longer acceptable. We are ready for something radically different. Because Aquarius is not bound by commonly held beliefs, and because of its innate curiosity and openness to thinking and being outside the box, this new climate is ideal for the emergence of bold, new, radical ideas, teachings and possibilities.

While today's messages are similar in meaning to those given to us by Jeshua 2000 years ago, they are being brought forth in different styles, through a wide variety of channels, as well as from beings from other dimensions and galaxies. These forms of communication are most appropriate for the vibration and climate of Aquarius, given that this is the Age that gave rise to the science fiction and space exploration genres. Teachings are also being shared in today's language, using metaphors and images that are more relatable and that are especially devoid of the aggressive, fear-based, disparaging, authoritarian, judgmental, male-dominated intonations carried forward from the low-consciousness mindset of the previous Eras.

Many are realizing that there is simply far too much emotionality, confusion, divisiveness, competitiveness, hate, greed, dishonesty and conflict in the world at this time. The drama that has flourished for eons will not be sustained in the calm, logical, rational climate of Aquarius. Nor will inequality, senseless control measures, threats to individual freedoms, social and cultural hierarchies and the imposition of unfounded beliefs. All of this just doesn't feel good, and now feeling—an invaluable trait of Aquarius—is being used as a valid tool for determining what is right and what is worthy of one's attention. Given our growing desire to know the truth, and given the radical nature of the information being revealed in new teachings, humanity is in the best possible timeframe for bringing about groundbreaking change.

A Century of Great Transformation

The next century will be a period of tremendous transformation for humanity. As can be seen by the upcoming transits of the three outer planets, there will be much activity in the signs associated with the previous Eras, Pisces, Aries and Taurus, as well as in the newly emerging Era of Aquarius. Contrary to the apparent backward direction of the precession of the equinoxes, the orbits of the planets in the solar system trace a forward movement through the twelve signs of the zodiac. As Uranus, Neptune and Pluto bring their energies to this sector of the sky over the next hundred years, we will have the opportunity to bring to light, correct and clean up what was learned and acquired during the Eras of Pisces, Aries and Taurus. This will prepare the way for establishing a new journey for humanity, allowing for a higher-consciousness Aquarius climate to emerge.

CHAPTER 12 • A NEW BEGINNING

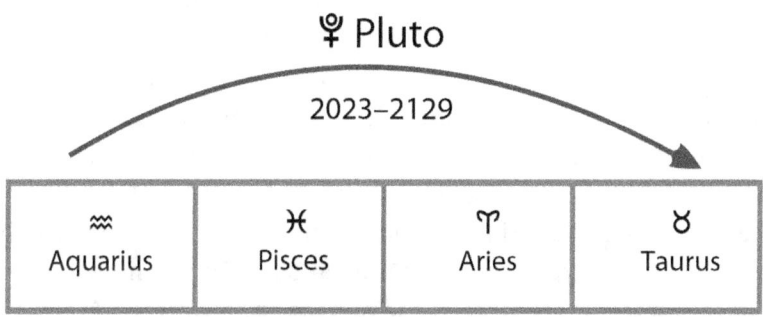

Uranus, the ruler of Aquarius, completes its orbit around the Sun in approximately 84 years. It brings energies of radical change, innovation, freedom, intuition and bold new ideas. Neptune, the ruler of Pisces, completes its orbit in approximately 164 years. It brings energies that allow the breaking down and dissolving of barriers and boundaries, preparing the way for unlimited possibilities.

Pluto, the planet associated with profound transformation, will be spending the entire period transiting through this significant sector of the sky. In 2023, Pluto will make its first entry in Aquarius, the sign of its exaltation, where it operates at its strongest. Here, it will provide opportunities for significant shifts of consciousness, learning and understanding. Over the next 100 years, it will continue to travel through the sector of the sky that covers Aquarius, Pisces, Aries and Taurus. Pluto takes approximately 248 years to complete its orbit around the Sun. However, given the eccentricity of its orbit, the time spent in each sign varies from 12 to 33 years, with an average of about 21 years. Pluto was known as the god of the underworld and is associated with the collective unconsciousness, revolution and regeneration. Like the surgeon, it pulls out the cancer that stands in the way of perfect health and wholeness, and so it holds the power of great transformation.

The last time Pluto transited Aquarius (1777–1798), the world saw several revolutions where the common people began to claim freedom from outdated political and dictatorial forms of rulership. In its highest form of expression, Aquarius is the sign of "every man/woman," brotherhood and sisterhood, equality, sovereignty, community and sharing. Above all, it seeks freedom of expression. It is non-hierarchical and humanitarian and will accord the same opportunities for all. From 2023 to 2044, Pluto will once again travel through Aquarius, providing unlimited opportunities for bringing about great transformation and healing for humanity.

The upcoming transits of the outer planets through Aquarius, Pisces, Aries and Taurus will be like waves from the Ocean of Life flowing over the shoreline of our tiny, made-up, illusory island of separation. For humanity, these waves will serve to remove all distortions, errors, misconceptions, limitations and boundaries that stand in the way of a full experience of our divinity. A clean slate is being prepared so we can rise up, reclaim our true Self and once again function in peace, harmony and Oneness. Free of the burdens of the past and ready to explore the new, we will come to reknow ourselves as high-consciousness creator beings.

The desire to live in a world where everyone is out for everyone rather than just out for themselves seems like a big ask at this time. However, this is what we must ask for, this is what we must aim for and this is what we must now choose. Being out for self alone will no longer be sustainable because it is not natural and does not reflect who we truly are. We are beginning to know and understand that the small self must eventually be relinquished since it is founded on the illusion of separation. Individually, tiny drops of water can do little, but joined in the flow of an ocean wave, they become all-powerful. Oneness is the most powerful force of all, and it will cause all division to fade from the human experience. By working together as a community, as a family, which is very much at the heart of higher-consciousness Aquarius, we will uncover our full creative power.

CHAPTER 12 • A NEW BEGINNING

A Test of Our Desire for More

We can spend a lifetime studying the history of humanity, but since history books are generally written by the conqueror, someone who is still bound by the limited perception of the small self, we would not have a complete picture of our past. Besides, we don't need to look too far back to identify the level of consciousness being expressed by the human collective. The recent worldwide crisis known as the "COVID-19 pandemic" will have been a life-altering learning opportunity for all of humanity, in particular for today's youth. One can only wonder if the youth of today will be as idealistic as the youth of the 1960s. What will they have learned during this period of crisis? Will they be inspired to break from the past and embrace a new way for humanity? Or will they sink lower into the dream state, clinging to the illusion of separation, looking for ways to avoid what needs to be done.

The way in which the pandemic was handled is like a caricature of the level of consciousness held by humanity at this time. Fear and drama (Pisces) were used as the major driving forces throughout this time, making it easier to apply control measures by those holding positions of power. The divisiveness inherent in the state of separation was then augmented through social distancing, the wearing of masks, the absence of physical contact and self-isolation. Further divisiveness ensued between those who obeyed the regulations and those who refused to do so. Many people made a lot of money (Taurus) from the sale of vaccines (Neptune), "protective gear," and essential goods and services. And, of course, there were those individuals, cities, states and countries who competed (Aries) for vaccines and necessary equipment. Social media, electronic and communication devices (Aquarius) were used extensively to disseminate an overabundance of information leading to further confusion and divisiveness.

The collective response to this crisis was like a desperate cry from those clinging to the low-consciousness energies of the previous Eras, those who were not ready to release the old ways and experience a new way of being. It was like saying: hey, wait, we can't go forward into this new Era; it's too frightening, we don't know what it will be like, and we don't know what it will cost. We don't want to lose our current benefits and advantages, no matter how limiting they may be. We're willing to engage in fear and continued divisiveness just to make sure we don't experience something we're not entirely familiar with, like peace, healing and unity.

If the virus situation had been addressed from a higher level of consciousness, there very likely would have been far fewer deaths and much less illness. There may not even have been a pandemic in the first place. Millions of people would have come together with a mindset of love and wholeness, generating powerful healing energies around the globe. The healing powers of plants would have been used, and healthy immune-enhancing foods would have been provided for all. The spirit of love, unity, inclusiveness and a sense of service for family and community would have prevailed. With these wise and enlightened measures, the virus would likely have been eliminated in a very short amount of time. Those who were ready to leave the planet at this time could have done so in a peaceful and even joyful manner, celebrating their precious life opportunities with their loved ones.

As creators of our reality, we must have brought this major event into our collective experience, and so its sole purpose must have been to test our desire for change. Do we truly want to claim our higher Self, or do we want to adhere to our old familiar lower consciousness small self? At every moment throughout this challenging period, we had the opportunity to choose for fear and divisiveness, to engage in hatred, judgment, frustration and anger, or to choose for the higher level option of love, caring, understanding, light, healing, wisdom and unity. How we personally addressed the situation can help us understand where we, individually, stand in terms of our own level of consciousness. Just like any other life event, this has been a wonderful learning opportunity for each and every one on the planet. Having learned, now we move on.

CHAPTER 12 • A NEW BEGINNING

The Journey Begins

We can begin by expressing gratitude and appreciation for this beautiful planet that is our host, for the abundance of goods that it provides us (Taurus). It is time for us to use our industry and initiative to build a world and communities that include all of our brothers and sisters (Aries). It is time for us to share our love for everyone, to live in peace and to be from Love eternal (Pisces). It is time to get rid of anything that keeps us from experiencing the higher level of consciousness of which we are capable and let in the spirit of love and wholeness that we are. Being open to the new and engaging in simple curiosity (Aquarius) will be a powerful driving force in the years to come.

Those who are waiting for a golden age of love, light and peace to magically appear on Earth are enjoying the illusion of a foolish, empty, ego-based promise. Although our wholeness remains always available and has never been taken away from us, in order to bring about a golden age, we will need to consciously re-establish our relationship with our true Self. This means that we do not need to wait for anyone or anything outside of us before we can shift to a higher level of consciousness. Given the depth of our current state of sleep or our firm identification with a limited version of ourselves, this shift will not occur without a little work on our part—okay, maybe a lot of work. How far are we willing to go, and what are we willing to do to make the world a better place for ourselves and for all life on the planet?

As we stand at the portal between Pisces and Aquarius, many are starting to recognize that a world devoid of Oneness is not sustainable. A world without Love is not one in which we want to live. A world of boundaries and limitations is no longer acceptable. Reclaiming our inherent Oneness will allow us to express our true greatness. Through our experience of shared Love and Unity, together we will find our true power as creator beings. True power comes from joining as a whole, in allowing for the experience of the Oneness of humanity, in the same way that the infinite Source of life is all-inclusive and does not favour one of its expressions over another.

We now understand that we live in a world of our own making, modelled on the long-standing beliefs we hold about ourselves and about the world. This may or may not be taken as good news, at least not at first, but it will need to be accepted if we are to move forward on our journeys of awakening. The upside is that we are now aware of the fact that, as creator beings, we have the freedom to make new and different choices. More importantly, we have the power to bring about significant change. True power will be accessed when we consciously choose to join with and listen to the true Self, our innate connection to Mind, God/Source. True power is never overwhelming; it is harmonious, balanced and flows naturally. True power inspires expressions that are inclusive, kind, peaceful, healing, enlightening, beautiful, creative, loving and supportive. This is what we need to express in our shift into the New Age.

We can use this transition time to release the old, to experiment and engage in a little R&D, make improvements, and try new ways of being with ourselves and with each other. Since this shifting of our consciousness to a higher level is new—or this is how it seems at the beginning—it won't be perfect at first, so mistakes will be made. And that's okay since the truth of what we are has never been altered. Change will emerge as we learn to tap into the inspiration, wisdom and creativity of the higher Self, that aspect of us that is calling for change. As we learn to listen to the inner voice, intuition or guidance, we will know which actions to take, where to go, which choices to make. When aligned with the true Self, simply asking for help from guidance will bring it into our experience. All that is needed is to be open and to allow it to come into awareness.

While the initial spark comes from deep within us, we do come to learn that this is not a journey undertaken alone, nor is it undertaken for our sole benefit. Fortunately, we are not alone, and we have help from guides and those who have answered our calls—lots of help! As we explore this radical shift in consciousness, we come to understand that, as integral parts of something far greater than

CHAPTER 12 • A NEW BEGINNING

what we have for so long believed ourselves to be, this journey is undertaken for the benefit of all. Since inclusiveness, friendship and community are among the wonderful traits of high-consciousness Aquarius, the journey is filled with hope, joy and wonder.

As we raise our level of consciousness, separation will be set aside and we will remember and *know* what it is like to be One with the Whole of Creation. As we allow and embrace our return to Oneness, situations and circumstances in our lives will be transformed, and since there can only be harmony in Oneness, more harmony will be experienced in the world around us. In Oneness, true Love is experienced, and everyone and everything we encounter is also known and loved.

For our return to wholeness to be achieved, only the desire is required. Since wholeness is our natural condition, once the desire has been expressed, what is needed for our healing will simply come into our life. Because we have called for the truth, the pressure that resulted from maintaining the illusory small self is disappearing. Since time is only relevant on the limited, 3-D body/mind level, as we rise to higher dimensions of experience, the entire cycle of the Eras will fade from our experience and be replaced by something new and far more uplifting and enlightened. By claiming our true Self, even our individual astrological signatures will no longer be needed, for they but serve as learning devices, garments of sorts, bringing to us those circumstances needed for our growth.

As we explore new possibilities for humanity, the tiny, made-up island of separation fades away. Gradually, we return to Oneness, where an infinite Ocean of possibilities emerges, where we can access the true power of Mind, energy, vibration, soul, spirit, love, beauty, light, joy, harmony, peace, truth, infinite creativity—all that is our true birthright. In time, our experience will shift, and since we are creator beings, the changes we choose to bring forth will create a new world, a different experience for all, one that reflects our wholeness, perfection, love, wisdom and innate connection with Source.

An Invitation

Dear Brothers and Sisters

Please accept this invitation to be the Presence of Love. It is a one-time invitation, but due to its divine nature, it will never expire. You may accept it now, you may ignore it awhile, or you may reject it outright, but you cannot destroy it. It will always be there as it has always been there. It is a seed planted in the fertile soil of your Soul, and since the substance of your Being is Love, it cannot be destroyed. When you are ready, it will germinate and blossom, for unbounded expression is its very nature.

This is an invitation to release all grievances and ancient hurts. There is no cost other than the cost of abandoning resistance to Love. It will require the relinquishment of all forms of resentment, grievance, condescension, hatred, anger, judgment, disdain, bitterness, antagonism, hurt, defensiveness and self-righteousness, but, what a small price to pay in comparison to the burden of clinging to and sustaining long-held destructive, painful, hurtful and unloving sentiments.

At first glance, this invitation may seem impossible to accept but, in truth, there is nothing simpler. In fact, it is not natural for your being to be expressing anything but love; to be expressing anything but love can only be uncomfortable and most unsatisfactory. If you have forgotten what the nature of love is, here are some reminders: love is always appropriate. It is kind, it judges not, it is gentle but firm when necessary, it is intelligent, it recognizes itself in another, it is nurturing, healing and infinite. To come from love is to come from your true Self. Love waits simply for your acceptance.

There is no need to worry that there will not be enough to go around. Love need not—nor can it—be measured, for it grows without end as it is shared. There are no limitations to love, for it is infinite. The rewards of coming from a place of love are immeasurable; they can only be experienced, and as they are experienced, more love will be expressed. Because being the Presence of Love is natural, it is healing for yourself and for everyone you encounter every minute of every day of your life. Above all, it feels good, an experience that is very much in harmony with the higher consciousness of Aquarius.

Thank You

Okay, so I've actually finished writing yet another book. It's time to switch keyboards. I need some music medicine. Which song should I start with? I have such a long wishlist of songs to learn! I think I will start with "God Bless the Child."

Thank you, dear reader, and God bless you for sharing your light on this journey. Together, we are contributing to the shift to a higher level of consciousness for all of humanity.

A New World

Imagine just for a moment
What a new world would look like
A world redeemed from hell
And instead being the Heaven it was created to really be
Imagine things working out for you and everyone else, too
Solutions to long-held problems finally appearing
Beautiful, loving people and animals,
Wonderful natural beauty of rivers and lakes,
Forests and mountains, gardens of delight
Soul-stirring music and beautiful art
The idea we are in the mind of God
Bringing forth perfect mental and physical health
Harmony between all people
And serenity within as we reintegrate our wholeness
Abundance for all as we finally learn to share and care
No one left out of a love that can't be contained
As the cup of joy spills over
Nothing that couldn't be done, dream big!
Interstellar flight and teleportation
Incredible new worlds to explore
An infinity and eternity of always new, awe-inspiring experiences
Deep, nourishing peace
Love and perfection bursting forth from every place and being
An end to aging and death!
This is indeed what waits for all of us
If we would only love ourselves and others,
As our Creator and Source loves us all!
Child of God, the pure, the holy, the good, break free!

Michael J. Miller

Bibliography

A Course in Miracles. Sparkly Edition.

Bach, Edward. *Free Thyself.* Mount Vernon: The Bach Centre, 2014.

Carroll, Lee. (channeller for Kryon). www.kryon.com.

Coates, Judith. *Jeshua: The Personal Christ,* Volumes I–VII. Oakbridge University Press.

———. Jeshua Online—Daily Messages.

Edward, Pauline. *Making Peace with God: The Journey of a* Course in Miracles *Student.* Montreal: Desert Lily Publications, 2009.

———. *Choosing the Miracle.* Montreal: Desert Lily Publications, 2012.

———. *Astrological Crosses: Exploring the Cardinal, Fixed and Mutable Modes.* Montreal: Desert Lily Publications, 2013.

———. *The Movement of Being.* Montreal: Desert Lily Publications, 2014.

———. *The Healing of Humanity.* Montreal: Desert Lily Publications, 2017.

Grun, Bernard. *The Timetables of History: A Horizontal Linkage of People and Events.* New York: Touchstone/Simon and Schuster, 1982.

Meece, Alan. *Horoscope for the New Millennium.* St. Paul: Llewellyn, 1997.

Peterson, Barry. *Giving Voice to the Wisdom of the Ages* (YouTube channel).

Scranton, Daniel (channeller). *Ascension: The Shift to the Fifth Dimension, The Arcturian Council.* Volumes 1–3.

Selig, Paul. *I Am the Word.* Penguin Random House, 2010.

Spalding, Baird T. *Life and Teaching of the Masters of the Far East,* Volume 1. Marina Del Rey: DeVorss & Co., 1964.

About the Author

Pauline Edward is an astrologer-numerologist, speaker, Certified Professional Coach and Group Leader. She is the recipient of a Chamber of Commerce Accolades Award for excellence in business practice. With a background in the sciences and a fascination for all things mystical, Pauline's journey has been enriched by a wide range of experiences from research in international economics, technical writing in R&D and computer training, to studies in astrology, numerology, meditation, yoga, spirituality, shamanism, the Bach Flower Remedies, herbology, healing and reiki. Her profound desire to uncover the truth about the meaning of life was the inspiration behind her lifetime of writing.

Pauline is available for speaking engagements and workshops. For information about services, upcoming events and publications, visit her website: www.paulineedward.com.

Reviews

As kindred spirits and friends for some years, Pauline and I have shared a common desire and many late night conversations pondering why we are on this planet at this time. We have both on many occasions said, "What would I do without you to exchange all our weird ideas."

Pauline has written many books but this one is different. In the past few years many new, exciting, and uplifting teachings have come into our awareness. She was yet again nudged to put pen to paper and come out of her monk cave and comfort zone (her words) and write about her two passions, astrology and awakening.

Pauline has so effectively, as only she can, in a clear, concise and simplified manner, without all the jargon, managed to marry two subject matters that are considered by many as too complex and difficult to grasp. Witnessing Pauline share her personal stories, which I know was not an easy task, is a testament to her desire and determination to get her work out into the world.

Pauline's book is an invitation for those of us who are demonstrating a little willingness and curiosity to embrace a different way to contribute to new possibilities in a new Era for humanity. I am extremely grateful for her courage and to be able to share this path together.

Helena Basso

Pauline's latest book clarifies our Oneness in an easy and understandable way, and is spot-on for our times in the 2020s when the healing of humanity and being IN love can bring us to the level of our awakening. I particularly enjoyed the personal experiences shared and the exercises to use (I can personally attest that the exercises work). Looking forward to reading more from Pauline, when she has finished experimenting in the kitchen, playing piano and feeding the ducks.

Elizabeth Luik

Pauline's new book, her sixth in her awakening series, shows her growth as a writer and especially as a person. She has worked hard and it has borne wonderful, life-giving fruit. There is much here for your own growth and healing, from self-love to tapping into the Higher Self to the releasing of judgment. She places our personal journeys in the context of the shift of Eras from Pisces to Aquarius and what's shown is a message of hope and possibility for nothing less than the awakening of humanity to its true potential. An inspiring work to read and reread. Well done, Pauline!

Michael J. Miller

Pauline's latest book reminds us of who we really are and who we can really be. This book is easy to understand and simplifies many abstract concepts. Every time I picked up this book, it brought me back up to myself, back to LOVE and growth.

Camille Greenstein, R. Ac. PTS, RYT-400